Praise for *Home Again and Again:*

"The author's incredible gift for storytelling and a topic that we can all relate to make this book both enjoyable and inspirational. I was captivated by the people and stories of her past and the variety of settings that contributed to making people and places 'home.' Ann's sensitive and inquisitive nature and remarkable memory helped create a book that would be a delight to discuss with a book club. I can hardly wait!"

–**JUDY SNOW NATIONS**, author of *Quite the Journey* and *Men of the Holidays*

"The personality of the author is evident. The words and phrases that come to mind are spontaneous, engaging, playful, creative, devout, loyal, whimsical, comfortable with herself, integrated, and having an excellent sense of humor."

–**RON POTTER-EFRON**, MSW, PhD, author of *Letting Go of Anger*, and *Being, Belonging, Doing; Balancing your Three Greatest Needs* and more

ISBN: 979-8-9855031-6-6

Printed, bound, and distributed by IngramSpark.

Cover Design by Caleigh Cleary
Illustrations by Emily Heling
Interior Design by Caleigh Cleary and Emily Heling

Book design, editorial, and proofreading services provided by Hard-Penned Press
an imprint of The Teaching Press at UW-Green Bay
University of Wisconsin-Green Bay
2420 Nicolet Drive, Green Bay, Wisconsin, 54311-7001
uwgb.edu/teaching-press
teachingpress@uwgb.edu

HOME AGAIN AND AGAIN

Dr. Ann Gentry Recine

Louis Recine

For our children and grandchildren

Contents

The Way Home

Afterword

Acknowledgments

Forgiveness Handout

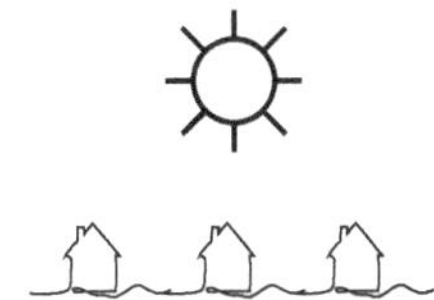

Introduction

I have tried to capture the lightning of love in a bottle with these stories about homes and neighborhoods in the heartland of Wisconsin, Illinois, and New England. Whether it turns out that I have done that, these pages will show. Most of these stories took place in Madison and Eau Claire, Wisconsin, but are a tribute to beloved homes across the land and beyond the sea. As it turns out, my Wisconsin tale begins in Illinois.

Tragedies happened in the little green house at 1603 Chevy Chase Drive, Champaign, Illinois, in the 1950s. Minor tragedies included our 2-year-old sister washing all the toothbrushes in the toilet, the huge misunderstanding as to whether or not Mom had said we could play in the mud puddle, and when Chicken Pox struck so I had to stay in the house on the very day that every kid in the neighborhood was in our backyard to watch the septic tank being cleaned out.

Real tragedies also came. Such as when my dad woke my brother and me in the night, and we knelt together and prayed that our new baby sister, Angela, who was in the hospital, would live. But she died.

Yet, though my first encounter with death and sickness was in this place, it was still a heavenly place to me.

Home is a place to which the people making the home turn back again and again when life throws them off track. They are turning back to aiming at making this place a heavenly place in sickness, health, life, and death.

"Minor tragedies included our 2-year-old sister washing all the toothbrushes in the toilet . . ."

I have a vocation and an avocation. My vocation has been as a primary care provider, science writer, and teacher of pathophysiology and pharmacology to doctoral students at the University of Wisconsin–Eau Claire, but my avocation is homemaking. At the height of the women's movement in the '70s, homemaking was sometimes disparaged. I read that the activities of homemaking could be done by the average 9-year-old. So it was that my fascination with all things home became my secret. Since then, I've come to understand that the importance of home is not just for women but for everyone: for all humans, no matter their circumstances. I'm coming out of hiding.

In 2022, some people did a huge study that shows us that it is not just elderly people who, because of the deaths of loved ones, are lonely. Since the 1970s, young people emerging into adulthood have been finding a fragmented society in which it is difficult to make the social connections that give them a sense of home. In this book, I share beautiful models of people who have shown me the way to make a home. These chapters, mostly set in Wisconsin, show us the way home through personal, family, neighborhood, and community stories of hospitality, not just in our houses but in unexpected places. This is mostly a book of true accounts about the beautiful. As Victor Hugo told us in *Les Misérables*, "The beautiful is as useful as the useful . . . perhaps even more so." Yet, since I am a science writer and teacher by profession, these pages offer some science-based guidance for healing our connections.

Just so you know what to expect, these stories are not in a strict chronological order. It is rather like opening up the little windows of one of those advent calendars we send to children. One window has a sheep, and one window has a cow, and by the time all the different little windows are open on December 24, we see the whole picture of the first Christmas. In the case of this book, the whole picture is of *Home*. And for those who like reading a book with a journal in hand to write down thoughts or with a group to discuss them, there are discussion questions at the end of the chapters to help you open the window of each chapter so as to shed light on your own home or life.

There are a few stories here about students, patients, and others whose anonymity is important. Though these are true to their core experience, I have changed the names and some details, and, in some instances, a composite is made to protect their privacy. All other stories are to the best of my memory. The re-created conversations are true in spirit.

WISCONSIN IS MY HOME

1

Surprised by Wisconsin

My mother was famous for short, funny stories that brought a laugh, no matter how often she told them. She frequently told the one about waking up in the morning in May of 1970 to a startling, impressive mess in the kitchen (from an art project I was doing for school and a little baking) and a wild teenage excuse for leaving it. My mom stood in the kitchen with curlers in her hair, in her flowered seersucker bathrobe. With her hands on her hips, she sharply said, "Why didn't you clean up all this dye, fabric, melted wax, and baking mess last night?"

As I was wolfing down my bowl of Grape-Nuts and raisins before school, I said, "I was expecting the house to be burned down, so it didn't seem worth it." That May was a time of great unrest and protest on the University of Wisconsin–Madison campus, and our home address, along with many other university administrators' home addresses, was posted on flyers all over the campus with the heading, "Bomb the Pigs!"

In 1969, when I was 16 years old, we moved to Madison, Wisconsin, from our New England home in a small town outside Cambridge, Massachusetts. I lost the bedroom I loved with its gold and white fleur-de-lis wallpaper and view of the sunrise over the spires and roofs of Winchester, Massachusetts. We moved because my father was leaving his job at Harvard. He was offered a job at the University of Wisconsin–Madison as the Associate Vice President for Business and Finance, perhaps because he had an excellent reputation from conferences he taught around the country. That meant I was going to move, at age 16 (the summer before my senior year in high school), from the metropolitan area of Boston to the "boring" Midwest. I worried I was moving somewhere unsophisticated and rural, but Madison was an impressive international and intellectual hub.

I stood at the entrance of Madison West High's noisy cafeteria on the first day of school in my sky-blue paisley dress (that had been sewn for me by a high school friend in New England) and light brown leather boots (that I had picked out on a shopping trip with another high school friend). I stood there, missing Winchester and high school classmates, feeling lonely, and wondering if I would make new friends. As I looked out at the sea of busy, laughing teenagers eating with each other, I doubted there was any room in their lives for me. But, by the end of September, I had experienced the famous Midwest friendliness. My new best friends—Dave, Rusty, Linda, Phoebe, and Jep—welcomed me into their lives and their families' homes. They loved me as only teenagers can.

Soon, my new friends, Pragmatic Phoebe and Laughing Linda, were marching down State Street with me and crowds of people holding candles, chanting peace slogans, waving two-finger peace signs, and singing anti-war songs like "Blowin' in the Wind" and "Give Peace a Chance." It was a beautiful night in November of 1969 when the famed folk band, Peter, Paul, and Mary came to Madison. Peter and his family stayed at Linda's house. They played concerts at the Coliseum and the University Ecumenical Religious Center and invited students to a war moratorium in Washington D.C. to non-violently protest the war in Vietnam.

About Peter and his family staying at Linda's house: her mom, a member of the Wisconsin State Assembly, a mother of five boys of military draft age, and a leader in the nonviolent anti-war movement, had invited him to her home to help Madison bring our boys home from the war, and had organized a few extra gigs for him to fundraise.

When we moved to the Midwest, our family's life changed. But not because it was boring compared to the Boston area. The night I decided it was not worth it to clean up the kitchen, a mob of angry students was marching down University Avenue toward our neighborhood, and the police were aware of the bomb threat to our address. This night was less than a year after we moved to "God's country" (as my mother called it). Nowhere was God's country in May of 1970, after students were shot dead protesting the Vietnam War at Kent State University in Ohio and Jackson State University in Mississippi. Madison, like other campuses, exploded with violence and firebombs, and thousands of students took to the streets.

When I famously decided I didn't want to clean up the kitchen that night, my dad had just told me that a dear older man I had met, a retired university administrator, had his beautiful old home bombed—injuring his 4-year-old grandson! My father, an experienced contract negotiator, had recently negotiated with "the feds" for Harvard on the moon-shot research in 1969. He was called into service to negotiate a contract between the National Guard, the University Police, and the Madison Police to try to keep the peace and respond to the rioting. My dad told me that bloody, injured police and students frequently filled the university hospital emergency room, and his job was to get order back in the streets.

It was a weird surprise that my father, who opposed the Vietnam War and was an independent, moderate thinker, whose father had been asked by Roosevelt to be part of his cabinet during WWII, had come under the ire of a mob of students—because of a position he held at the university. My father, who had spent hours on long walks explaining to me the importance of Martin Luther King Jr.'s work, was a target of violent threats! Like Reverend King (who had been shot the spring of my sophomore year in high school), he believed that a humble and loving spirit was needed in our country to make the necessary changes to combat the evils of our time. I longed for a different, more peaceful world, especially when the students marched down University Avenue toward our neighborhood.

Everyone who was in Madison knows precisely where they were on August 24, 1970, at 3:42 a.m., just like when Kennedy was shot. It felt like an earthquake when a blast in the middle of that summer night shook my bedroom. Sterling Hall (the math-science building) was bombed, and 33-year-old Robert Fassnacht, a postdoctoral researcher, died in the blast. Ironically, he opposed the Vietnam War and wasn't doing military research.

The bombed building was near the university hospital, and phones began ringing all over Madison, waking the hospital employees. Off-duty staff were called to come into the hospital to pull glass out of the patients since the windows shattered and blew into the rooms. It was a time of upheaval and transformation in 1970 when the peace movement was shaken as we saw the rubble. FBI agents in business suits picked through the remains of the building and canvassed Madison for clues about the perpetrators. Some leaders of the anti-war movement fled Madison in fear of arrest. Many parents suddenly withdrew their children from the university and drove to Madison to move them home from the dorms. That was not my parents' approach, which seems reasonable because the dorms may have been safer than our family's home address.

I was 17 and accepted into the university for the semester about to start. My math class was going to be in the part of the math-science building still standing. I would have to walk on a depressing path through that rubble, bordered on either side by yellow police tape. I wondered how shell-shocked my math teacher was going to be. After walking through the halfway demolished building and sitting in my first class with a young, pale-faced teacher putting equations on the blackboard, I walked straight to the administration building and filled out a drop-slip; I simply felt too shaken inside to imagine learning anything about math in that classroom. I wanted a different world. I had more than the usual angst that comes from starting college. I had fear about my tomorrows as I began the semester, walking through tear gas on Bascom Hill, by boarded up windows on State Street, and over broken glass as I went to buy my books and start classes.

"Our homes can be messy places of minor and major tragedies. Yet, there are little ways each day that people have always found to bring elements of heaven to our earthly home."

I wandered around the outdoor seating at the Memorial Union terrace on campus, overlooking Lake Mendota, and found a seat alone at a table. A grad student from Israel sat down at the table and began a conversation. We talked about our goals and longings for a peaceful future. As we talked about the tensions in the world, I listened as he told me that solutions could be found in world history. Then, taking my mailing address, he promised to send me a book that explained the solutions to our time from history. His idealism was contagious. Through this conversation on the terrace, he helped me to see human history as a large, strong tree (like an oak) with branches that stood, offering something to our time. Our time, which made my head feel like a weather vane in a tornado, needed a transformation. To me, the branches of history pointed in so many directions, but what gave me hope was the green sap and the strength within the tree that pulled life from the mud, drawing it heavenward toward the stars. He was the son of Holocaust survivors and showed me that the human spirit pointed away from the mud to the sky. His words gave me hope.

Even though I was unsure about what I believed from my upbringing, after listening to this highly articulate Israeli grad student, I could picture the hope Jewish people had in looking forward to a coming Messiah. I agreed it would be good to have someone come who could set this all straight. As I looked at the cloudless sky over the Memorial Union terrace and the reflection of the sun on the lake, in my 17-year-old imagination, I pictured a loving, compassionate, just, mighty leader who would come out of the sky—not to destroy and start a new world but to transform hearts, homes, and countries by love. He listened when I told him that I pictured this dystopia, with its death and violence that I was experiencing, transformed, inch by inch, into a good place that had elements of heaven.

Our homes can be messy places of minor and major tragedies. Yet, there are little ways each day that people have always found to bring elements of heaven to our earthly home. Some of these people I have talked about in this book. Some of these people are reading this book. This book is meant to be a tribute to the ordinary lives that transform our world into a home again and again. How do they transform our world? By constantly turning back to forgive one another, make apple pies, listen to one another, and make a home, office, hospital room, or university campus into a heavenly place in sickness, health, life, or death.

Or perhaps making chocolate chip cookies for a mob of angry students could help transform this dark and unheavenly world. My mom just rolled her eyes at my plan to conquer the angry students by baking them cookies. It would have been a catastrophe if the police and students converged on our family's house that night. But I had a desire to rescue my family and maybe even a few students and police officers. Warm chocolate chip cookies were my small offering to transform the evening.

Home Again Moment

Our lives can be filled with *big* and *small* "I did not see that coming" events. Sometimes, something seems to alter our lives beyond all hope of returning to the routine and comfort of "before." But is that just an illusion brought on by the shock we've sustained? Somewhere inside of us, in a quiet moment, we might sense that we *can* rise again. Sometimes, it's through that conversation with a caring person in our lives, or from the perspective gained by gazing at a beautiful sky, or . . . until eventually, we *can*, at least dimly for now, see a good life again in front of us. We can imagine *home* again.

Home Again Questions

What stood out, struck you, or moved you in this chapter?

What have been your go-to sources of inspiration, comfort, and strength when upsetting, even shocking, things have happened to you, and why?

For Further Reflection

Sometimes, in our grief or self-absorption, we can miss the hope, strength, or inspiration in our friends, environment, or the present moment.

2

Longing for Home

Home is a strong word, and homesickness is a strong, aching sickness, an invisible tugging in our hearts about all the things we are missing out on at home. When I had not quite turned 6, I had a bad case of FOMO—a fear of missing out—a deep ache.

Yes, in 1957, when I was a first grader, I knew that ache well. I won the privilege of being Mary in the first-grade Christmas pageant at Holy Cross School. Out of a classroom of 81 students, my teacher, a nun who dressed like the nuns in *The Sound of Music*, chose me because I had the most improved behavior. I improved by crying only *once* a day. When I started first grade, I spent the entire day quietly crying at my desk and not paying attention to my teacher because I longed to go home and be with my mother and sisters. I came by this honestly because my mother was also a refusenik in first grade, insisting on going home to be with her younger sisters. We knew that this was not home, and we just longed to go home.

✧✧✧

I went to college at age 17 at the University of Wisconsin–Madison, where my dad had an office on the 18th floor of the Van Hise Building, the tallest building on campus. I can't really say I moved away from home to go to college. During my first year, I lived in the dorms by Lake Mendota. But I wasn't far from home, only about a two-mile bike ride on the lake path by Picnic Point and through Shorewood to my parents' west side home. I lived there because my dad said, "A dorm is like a nest from which to hatch into adult life." I studied in his office with a view of the Madison skyline. During my sophomore year, I lived at home. Later, after my parents moved away from Madison to a university town, Carbondale, Illinois, I stayed in Madison and lived in a house of women near campus and the Vilas Zoo.

As a nursing student in the '70s, I was given a few addresses of people to visit for my public health clinical assignment. I was dropped off in an old neighborhood of bungalows with tidy yards in a nearby rural town, Waunakee, Wisconsin. It was a sunny early September morning. The modest homes looked so cozy, and though I don't remember being of any help to the patients as I visited their homes, I do remember that their homes spoke silently but very loudly to me.

The geraniums on the stoops, the curtains in the windows, and the cushions on the couches irresistibly called to me like the sirens called lost sailors to turn into a port in Greek mythology. I realized in my heart that I was at sea without a home port. Living with other women was an education since so many of them had been raised on Wisconsin farms and had skills I had never learned. They loved teaching me things like potting plants, making soup, and so on. Yet, when I got away from campus and stopped rushing to classes and gatherings of students and saw these cozy neighborhoods, I surprised myself by my longing. I longed for a home of my own with a husband, children, curtains, and geraniums.

☼☼☼

I recently mentioned this to a young man who comes to our house often for dinner. He is an unmarried single father in his 40s who has been a friend of our family since he began hanging out here in high school. In 2022 he moved back to Eau Claire, his hometown, to care for his father and is now setting up an apartment. He said that he has not really had a settled, safe sense of home since his nurturing parents divorced when he was in high school. He tried to make the apartment where he lived in another state a home for his daughter but never felt it was a home for him. He is an artist and a writer and longs to create a place that feels like home. His sister recently cozied up his little downtown Eau Claire apartment with some rugs and worked with him to assemble a shelf. He plans to add a beautiful piece of furniture he and his father made together at the birth of his daughter.

☼☼☼

What makes a place a home? It's a place that turns stuff into love. An inviting bowl of a variety of fruits on the dining room table, a soothing painting on the wall, and a bed cozily tucked under an alcove made under the stairs can be just stuff, or they can be light, love, and home.

There are people like those lost sailors of Greek myth who know what home is but have been set adrift, no longer settled in a home, no longer feeling at home in the world. Their need for sitting at a meal with congenial company in a relaxed home is a surprisingly strong longing. Tuning in to that longing in people is something my mother taught me. She had so many groups of people in for coffee, lunch, or card games because people need to have a place to come and be together. My mom was an unusually hospitable real estate agent. Once, she invited a man who had been house-hunting after his divorce to live with her and Dad for a few months before his house was ready. She explained, "He just needed someone to listen to him." She taught me to turn stuff into love: "It doesn't matter how simple what you serve is. People feel cared for if you serve it on pretty dishes and make a centerpiece."

Mom knew how to turn stuff like teapots and cookies into love for little neighbor kids and a meal of hot dogs or sloppy joes into a timeless memory. She turned stuff into love by welcoming everyone from lonely young priests to international students from other continents to our house for a homemade meal—showing love to people regardless of their intellectual frameworks about spirituality or politics through Chicken Divan and Lasagna. Before people were trying to address our polarized nation's longing for community with the "Make America Dinner Again" movement, my parents' dining table modeled warm, pluralistic hospitality where guests who needed a sense of home felt comfortable.

Budding entertainer Carol trying on Mom's
1949 U of I Homecoming Queen crown.

Recipe: Chicken Divan

Combine ½ cup of real mayonnaise, 1 can of Cream of Chicken Soup, ½ teaspoon of curry spice, and 1 teaspoon of lemon juice to make the sauce.

Spread a package of frozen chopped broccoli evenly across the bottom of a 9"x12" baking dish. Top with 2 pounds of chopped cooked chicken and cover with the sauce. Bake for 35 minutes at 350 degrees Fahrenheit.

Even my effervescent youngest sister, Carol, played the little hostess. Though it must have come as a surprise to the young Father Kelly and Father McDermitt to be regaled by the cherubic 6-year-old Carol, with her song of greeting, "Hello Dolly" (in her flawless Louis Armstrong impersonation, which occasionally was done standing on her head in the gravel driveway for dramatic effect). Though Father MacCasey was surprised at nothing since he knew our family (including our budding entertainer) so well. Smiley blond Carol was quite good at making our company feel at *home*. Once, she tried to help guests feel comfortable at our dining room table by reassuring them about the lasagna, telling them, "It looks icky, but it tastes good." She also thought this way when my mom made Chicken Divan. My recipe card for this is in Carol's handwriting with a few splashes of Chicken Divan on it.

I tried to follow Mom's lead and tune in to the longings of people who were adrift from a sense of home. One memory of this, which seems almost miraculous, happened on Christmas in the early 2000s. A young man, who was then a freshman in college at the University of Wisconsin–Madison, would come to stay with us in Eau Claire on school breaks. He told me that the only thing he wanted for Christmas was for his family to be together. He longed to be with both of his parents. Because his parents had recently divorced, he thought this couldn't happen at his dad's or mom's place. He asked if I could have his whole family over to our home for Christmas. I brought out a stack of old mismatched hymn books when they came over on Christmas Day. This gifted musical family sang every Christmas carol in the books in perfect harmony and pitch around our dining room table.

"6-year-old Carol, with her song of greeting, 'Hello Dolly' (in her flawless Louis Armstrong impersonation, which occasionally was done standing on her head in the gravel driveway for dramatic effect)."

People need a home. I might be an average cook at best, but my mom's life inspires me to aim with all my heart to make our home a place where anyone who crosses our threshold experiences *stuff being turned into love*.

Home Again Moment

Revisit in your imagination homes you've been in that have conveyed love. Some of the stuff in those homes transcended the material realm and conveyed love. It conveyed a message of "home" and fulfilled a longing.

Home Again Questions

What stood out, struck you, or moved you in this chapter?

How have you or someone you admire turned stuff into love for someone longing for home?

For Further Reflection

What is one small way you can turn stuff into love as you plan your week?

3

A University of Wisconsin Garden

"Most men walk on the street side of the sidewalk to protect their daughters from cars, but I think walking on the other side of the sidewalk protects you more. Rabbit attacks from the bushes are more probable," my dad explained as we walked along the sidewalk on University Avenue in Madison. That summer, I was 22 years old, had finally graduated, and was studying in the nursing library to take the board exam. My dad treated me to lunch every day. He would come from his office on the 18th floor of the Van Hise building on the University of Wisconsin–Madison campus to the medical library to pick me up, and we would take a leisurely walk through an elaborate campus flower garden by the agriculture school. My dad insisted that we stop, stand perfectly still, and pay as much attention to the little violets and pansies in the garden as to the roses and lilies. He insisted that he walk on the garden side of the sidewalk to protect me from aggressive bunnies.

After McDonald's fish sandwiches with tartar sauce, we would walk to get ice cream cones at Babcock Hall, the dairy that was part of the School of Agriculture. My father was from a long line of educated farmers. You might call them pig farmers since my great-grandfather Nicholas Hocker Gentry's portrait hung in the Chicago Stock Yard, honoring him as the wizard of the pig breeding world for producing the Berkshire Hog. My mom called them "Gentlemen Farmers." Maybe this is why Dad wanted me to know that the University of Wisconsin was founded by an agriculture grant and started as an agriculture school with a liberal arts emphasis.

My father used our walks together as an opportunity to instill his values into me. Spending so much time with my dad during my college years made every inch of the Madison campus feel like home. We would walk together, sometimes hand in hand, down the wide, steep historic Bascom Hill to the old Memorial Union for concerts, lectures, and lovely lunches.

He was passionate about the history of the university and what it meant to the people of Wisconsin. As we talked and walked together by the old, dignified brick buildings, I could picture the college in the 1800s when wolves roamed around the isthmus in Madison and the College of Letters and Science was founded. I imagined the farmers and immigrants of Wisconsin who built the university because they not only wanted their children to learn skills to become artisans in Wisconsin's workforce, but they also wanted their children to learn Greek, Latin, philosophy, the arts, and higher mathematics like young people in the East Coast schools like Harvard and Yale. (Mom liked to remind me that the country's four highest-rated schools were Harvard, Yale, Stanford, and the University of Wisconsin–Madison.) Dad helped me to see the connection between the college, our communities, and our homes.

One bright fall day, coming back from lunch at the old student union, as we walked along the lake path, shaded by pine boughs, he taught me about the *Wisconsin Idea*. "Annie, the university's mission is to reach beyond its campuses to make life better in Wisconsin and to inspire a search for truth." As I looked out at the shimmering lake full of a variety of boats, he explained, "Learning various subjects from many points of view helps us empathize with each other and connect. Learning about music helps us value musicians, and learning Wisconsin tribal history helps us empathize with what the tribes went through. Learning about scientific discoveries can inspire more discoveries and help everyone."

"My father used our walks together as an opportunity to instill his values into me."

Despite the theory that education was a glorious pursuit, I still have flashbacks of the horrors of nursing school: dissecting a human cadaver soaking in noxious formaldehyde, trying to adjust a microscope and correctly identify microorganisms with my astigmatism, reading dry research for hours, burning a hole in my clothes in a chemistry lab, and sitting in a lecture with hundreds of other kids. Sometimes, I didn't even know one of them by name. And there were a few teachers on my clinical sites who were impossible to please, no matter how much time I put into the preparation. Oh, and the clincher . . . I *hated* giving shots! By my senior year, I had decided that God had a plan for me, and it wasn't school.

"At this point, I'm just doing this for my parents," I told Gretchen, my fellow nursing student hoping for sympathy.

"Well, aren't we all?" she said.

"I'm quitting," I told my dad, and I meant it. I was determined to drop out. Unfortunately, one of the batons passed from generation to generation in the Gentry family is a firm educational foundation that enables children to earn a living, run a home economically, and become part of their community by participating in the arts. Later, my dad told me what agony he was in when I almost threw away my education in my senior year.

"If you reject education, you are rejecting me because *I am education*." I sighed when I heard my dad's response. Whether I was going to be a struggling violet of a nurse, planted on some small insignificant unit, or a rose of a nurse, I knew not. But I *was* going to be a nurse—not because I wanted to—but because my dad's loving attention was on all his children (intently and equally, like it was on the flowers blooming in the university garden). He was protecting each of us, not from a bunny attack but from an attack of hopelessness or loss of vision. God had a plan for me, and it was called "Dad."

"I am education"—my dad planting the seeds in me.

Home Again Moment

Who were the influencers in your life who have helped you to not quit when you were discouraged? How have they helped you to persevere?

Home Again Questions

What stood out, struck you, or moved you in this chapter?

Think back on a life path or course of endeavor in your life that you started, quit, and started again. Or, simply, a time you changed your mind about something important in your life. What moved you? What did you value that made the difference in your decision?

For Further Reflection

Were you ever in a relationship or situation where *you* were the person who urged someone else to reconsider a decision? Are you satisfied with how you went about it? If so, why? What would you do if you could go back in time and change your approach?

4

Madison Newlyweds' Home

September 10, 1977. Rented church.
Homemade gown. Happy couple.

"We don't know if you are compassionate or just cheap." Our friend Joyce said this because our first pet as newlyweds was a one-legged albino parakeet we got on sale. We named him A. B. Dick after an offset printer. Lou spent his inky workdays in a love affair with an A.

B. Dick printer at Econoprint on the west side of Madison, and it was nice to come home to our songful A. B. Dick and me.

It's possible we were an odd couple, at least an unexpected match to some. My husband Lou was from a first-generation Italian Chicago family who had come through Ellis Island in 1919. I was from an established family whose ancestors had come to settle in Jamestown in the 1600s, and I was raised off-campus at Big Ten and prestigious private universities. My dad asked me, "What do you have in common with him?" Not to give me something to ponder but because Lou was an unexpected fiancé. My dad couldn't see it.

When we met in 1974, I was longing for a husband who understood me and who I understood. I became friends with Lou, and we would go out to eat with our friends at the first Rocky Rococo pizza restaurant off State Street in Madison, Wisconsin. In one of our first conversations, he sat with me on a stairway at a friend's house and reproduced (with a ballpoint pen on lined paper in a spiral notebook for me to keep) a lesson he learned from his Lutheran pastor in youth group. I loved it. We were just friends. But I wondered if we could be more, so I asked to read his collection of spiral ring notebooks that were his diaries, complete with funny little drawings and poems he had written.

One Saturday, I sat reading them for hours while drinking free hot chocolate in the Newman Center on the UW campus in Madison. In that perch overlooking the passersby on State Street, reading his handwritten journals, I was moved by the emotional poems. I was touched by his diary drawings. I was in love. I decided he would make a good husband.

One evening, when we were on a walk, he held my hand. He was 19 years old and had never held a girl's hand. Looking back from the perspective of a woman who has been on this planet for 70 fallings of the leaves, I see that we were like babies. A few weeks later, he proposed to me while we were sitting on the steps of the Joyce Funeral Home on West Washington Avenue in Madison during an evening stroll.

After saying yes, I laughed and asked, "Where's the ring?" The next day, he showed me a ring he had dug out from his sock drawer for a joke. I insisted on wearing it even though it turned my finger green. I knew I had found a kindred spirit. We were soulmates with the motto, "From teenage to the grave." We took the ring to Middle Earth Silversmith and had them make a silver ring from the pattern. Lou was worried he was being cheap to give me a silver instead of a gold ring, but I assured him I loved it, "If it makes you feel better, you could give the extra money you would like to have spent on a fancier ring to a charity." When he placed the ring on my finger on September 10, 1977, our wedding day, I felt like Galadriel or Arwen in the Lord of the Rings with my ring of the promise of joy.

Yes, after a long engagement, during which Lou was working on getting a job that could support a family, we married on a sunny September day in a rented Methodist church near the University. The handmade lacey white wedding dress, made by my friend Jeannie, and the flowers a friend had arranged in my hair were things of beauty. Yes, even the cheap multicolored polyester bridesmaids' dresses were beautiful to us. We were supremely happy to be getting married as we walked down the aisle to the whole church, raising their voices to Bach's "Jesu, Joy of Man's Desiring." The rainbow of late summer flowers from the farmers market on the altar and the poignant guitar strains from friends helped make the day one of the most beautiful days of my life.

The after-party of family and friends was joy-filled even though we were eating an atrociously cheap menu of food I had carefully ordered to feed the most guests I could invite within my budget. (I cringe a little when I remember it, including very bland canned green beans and instant mashed potatoes.) The homemade carrot wedding cake my brother's friend made was the perfect topper. The total cost of the wedding was 500 dollars (donated by my dad), but it took. He was thankful for the price tag since putting four kids through college is not cheap.

Our first apartment was a cinder block efficiency (bedroom and combined kitchen, living room, dining room) near downtown Madison, Wisconsin. When our windows were open, sometimes, music wound its way through the nearby historic old archway, up through the trees, across Randall Avenue, and filled our home with the bracing songs of the University of Wisconsin marching band, conducted by Mike Leckrone. The band treated us to our own preview of the next football half-time show as the students practiced at Camp Randall Stadium a block away. Picturing Mike perched on his ladder surrounded by rookies and experienced players—I'd get shivers listening to the century-old song "On Wisconsin" (a tune so regal I would begin to expect a coronation at half-time). I would hum along with lyrics from another song they practiced to the tune of a Budweiser beer commercial as I made dinner in our little home.

"Another secret of our home was one we learned in kindergarten. We took turns."

We got around by riding old bicycles and buses. We were within biking distance from the Mifflin Street Co-op and an Italian grocery store, and that was all we needed. We were rich in friends but very poor in domestic skills, so the ambiance of this little bit of paradise was made by friends who realized that we needed to be taken under their wings to make a home. My friend, Jeannie, who was raised on a farm and knew how to do everything, helped me make the bedroom into a place of wonder. She used a mattress on the floor and wedding gift sheets hanging from the ceiling to create a canopy bed effect and helped me put up laminated art prints from museums on the cinder block wall. As we entered the bedroom and looked through the arch of the blue canopy at the wall, we felt the beautiful art of the centuries, like *The Blue Boy* by Gainsborough, transporting us to faraway places, and we experienced the joy of living.

I was lucky enough to have a Seventh-Day Adventist friend, Sarah. Maybe her mentoring in plant-based home cooking will help me and my family be lucky enough to live to 100 since later I found out (and taught my nursing students) that according to the Blue Zone research project, out of the homey lifestyles of Seventh-Day Adventists, especially the ones in Loma Linda, California, come the longevity superstars of America.

Sarah decided to teach me nutrition, cooking, and kitchen organization in my two-cupboard kitchen. She was a no-nonsense, primly dressed young woman who sewed all her own dresses. I met her while shopping at the Co-op. (I had a habit that I picked up from my father of talking to strangers and making new best friends everywhere I went.) She surprised me by not only being intent on improving my domesticity but in teaching me ancient history through spontaneous diagrams she would draw while the cookies were in the little oven, or the bread was rising. Her casual conversation about her fascination with ancient Jewish temple cooking of meats and bread gave a history class vibe to our cooking lessons. I never really could retain the historical details, but she did succeed in showing me how to fill my home full of sweet and savory smells and healthy food. She taught me the art of kneading whole grain bread at my tiny yellow Formica table while she asked my advice about saving her marriage. That advice was taken, and later, they brought a baby girl into this wonderful world. They named her Trixie. Yes, Trixie. She didn't ask my sage advice on that. I hope Trixie went to a middle school with kind children.

Anyway, Lou (covered in ink from his print shop job) would usually return from work to that little home with candles in the windows and who knows what amateur effort at Seventh-Day Adventist-inspired health food on the table. There was often deep discussion with wonderful friends around our little table. Once, after serving a meal to Lou and three other intellectual guys, the simple meal ended with a homemade whole wheat crust pie that needed a hammer and chisel to serve. Using whole grains in desserts can be tricky, yet the Mifflin Street Co-op whole wheat cupcake recipe, circa 1975, became a hit. It is the most food-stained recipe in my rusty yellow recipe box and was picked up in the days when the Co-op (run by college students) was one of the only places to get natural foods in Madison. Yes, the famous Co-op was not just known for radical politics and its yearly block party, but there were stacks of recipes for the taking amid the radical political flyers.

Recipe: Mifflin Street Co-op Whole Wheat Cupcakes (2 dozen)

Mix wet and dry ingredients separately, combine, then bake for about 20 minutes at 370 degrees Fahrenheit.

Wet: ¾ cup oil, 1½ cups honey, 2½ cups water,

½ teaspoon vanilla extract.

Dry: 4 cups whole wheat flour, ½ cup soy powder, 2 tablespoons baking powder, ¼ teaspoon baking soda, ½ teaspoon salt.

The almost 50-year-old treasured recipe card that I picked up from the beloved Co-op was a reprint of a student's handwritten card, complete with drawings of cupcakes, a teepee, and the shining sun. This was before students had personal computers or even, except in rare cases, personal typewriters. The back of the recipe card waxes lyrical about soy powder in cheerful hand-printing. An artifact from our happy, newlywed, low-tech, compact kitchen/living room.

We had a definite atmosphere of home there with the aroma of baking, our one-legged albino parakeet, our yellow plaid couch, and yellow curtains made from wedding gift sheets. Even my sewing basket and recipe box were yellow. A young couple from our apartment building, who had come to join us for one of my healthful homemade dinners at our yellow table and chairs, asked us to tell them our secret of happiness. They had trouble getting along because they would fight about how to fry potatoes. Should it be like his family did it, or like hers? They also tried to change each other's appearance. I think one of the secrets of our happiness was an obliviousness to how things ought to be done in the world of cooking and fashion.

Another secret of our home was one we learned in kindergarten. We took turns. For example, we took turns deciding what to do on our weekly dates. This helped us to keep growing in things in common. I read brain research suggested by Lou and Polish poetry (that I would never have thought of) to prepare for our date night over coffee or a beer. When it was my turn to choose, Lou learned to swim, skate, and even tried skiing.

And, of course, our mutual dedication to loving God was the secret. We had the philosophy that our relationship was like a triangle with a base in which Lou was on one corner, and I was on the other. We both were ascending our side of the triangle to the top, which was God. As we got closer to God, we got closer to each other. Lou tried to practice the simple truths he learned as a child from his gray, tattered copy of *Luther's Small Catechism*, which he brought to our bookshelf. Since the same ideals were part of my grade school curriculum, we were on the same page, inching or maybe stumbling toward the same goal of love.

Yet in spite of the general aura of happiness, sometimes, in that tiny efficiency apartment home, everything went wrong, and we were tossed from side to side like two seasick goldfish in a little jar. Lou got some kind of strange illness that the doctor misdiagnosed, and I got shigella with lots of pain, bleeding, and anemia. And there were important people we loved who didn't get us. But we just kept loving them (because they were so loveable). Lou's dad was perplexed by me because I broke all the unspoken rules that Italian women knew. He seemed to be on a campaign to re-raise me to be an Italian. I finally had a heart-to-heart with him after we had been married for a few years. I took him into a private room at his home and said, "I always leave here with my feelings hurt."

This 100 percent Italian man stood looking at me and started to weep. He knew I loved him. He said, "Anna, my parents put me through this, and now I am putting you through it. I am so sorry." I got it. His immigrant parents loved him and wanted to protect him and keep him safe in this new world where other Italian families were losing their kids to the mob, and banks were failing. Trying to make me act more Italian was his way of loving me, his son's new bride.

Our marriage involved a learning curve. We learned how to make a family even though our courtship had been like the couple in the movie *My Big Fat Greek Wedding*. We were from two very different cultures, with families that were very sure their way was best. Despite cultures colliding, or maybe because of it, we were learning to love. We are so glad that out of that love came two beloved human beings adored by both sides of the family. One we nicknamed Dodili, meaning beloved, and he was known as the littlest student on campus to our neighbors, who were almost all students. The other was a bundle of joy who lived up to her name, which means joy in Greek. She was a tiny grinner and a singer, especially when we played "The Weenie Roast" song on the record player and danced, wearing her in the snuggly front baby carrier. Even though you know that you will love your children, sometimes it surprises you how much! But as I came to find out, these experiences were only the beginning of more to come in my explorations of *home*.

Home Again Moment

"We were rich in friends." Sometimes, it is good to just stop and think about what a treasure your friends are to you, perhaps at the end of the day, when we think back on what we want to savor as we fall asleep. The friends in our family, our town, our school, and online are our greatest treasures.

Home Again Questions

What stood out, struck you, or moved you in this chapter?

What are some ways that you want to show your friends what they mean to you?

For Further Reflection

How can you show someone *in the next week's time* how much you treasure them? What are the practical steps needed to make this happen?

5

Homemaking at the University of Wisconsin–Eau Claire

I love to see each unique, and I am going to go ahead and say it, *precious* student walk across the stage to receive their diploma. I love to see them throw their caps in the air. They did it! Even though it was hard getting through some of those school days.

At 6:30 on a snowy January morning, on the first day of the first clinical experience of the eight nursing students in my group, we had a crisis. "Dr. Recine, Emily has fainted and hit her head." I hurried down the nursing home hall to find Emily in tears, sitting on the floor, rubbing her head, surrounded by seven other nursing students in crisp blue uniforms. "I'm so scared I will make a mistake giving the wrong pill or hurt my patient giving a shot." Anxious, worried, nervous, uncertain, and concerned—that is the understandable experience of many novice nursing students embarking on learning skills that can save lives or, if they make a mistake, kill someone.

Scared students would find their way to my door in the nursing building. When I heard a knock on my office door, I would often open the door to see the tears of a disappointed student who had studied all week but still got a C on the test or the flushed face of a frustrated student who was confused about the difficult immune system pathophysiology for the upcoming exam. They not only needed help understanding the material but were looking for hope, a calming presence, and an ear.

"My son's school called for me to pick him up because he was throwing up. I have some questions about the lecture I missed."

"It is so hard to sleep and to concentrate because my husband is deployed and hasn't called in days. Can I keep my phone on during class? It's his only window of time to make a call."

"I won't make it to clinical because my grandpa is dying, and I need to go home to be with him in the hospital. How can I make up the time?"

"Now I get you!" said a struggling, anxious young nursing student when she came for help to my tiny office (albeit with a window overlooking a hill of woods) in the College of Nursing at the University of Wisconsin–Eau Claire. Gabriella was not the first, the last, or the only student who introduced herself to me by telling me which anxiety disorder she had been diagnosed with. (Maybe because I taught the psychiatric content.) The level of perfection required in the grade-point average and resumés of nursing students resulted in some extremely intelligent but anxious learners.

Gabriella relaxed when she came into my snug little office. She said, "I think you need to add a couple of dollar store paper Chinese lanterns hanging from the ceiling to go with the vibe." She felt it would have added the right touch to the whimsy of the décor. It would go with the little round table with a teapot and cups in the corner, the Himalayan prayer flags, and the 40 or so beautiful greeting cards taped over the ugly nail holes in the cream-colored cement block walls. I had thrown these cards up as a temporary way to cope with an office that needed a paint job (that was not in the budget) with the suggestions and help of my old office mate and fellow doctoral student, whom I called Cindy Leprechaun-Whisperer (not her professional name). The décor was to be temporary but lasted until I retired at age 67. We did this decorating on the fly to celebrate that I got my own office after I graduated with my doctorate. Cindy made sure that she put a large sticky note on the edge of my computer screen in her writing, saying, "80/20." She had a note in my handwriting on her computer saying the same thing. This was to remind us to put 80 percent of our effort into the 20 percent of academia that was the most important and 20 percent of our effort into the rest.

The whole beautiful university campus felt like a home to me. I loved to get an omelet or sub at the Davies Center, where I could cozy up to one of their fireplaces in the dining area and hear the musical chatter of hundreds of students breaking for lunch at the food court. I loved to walk the wooded paths along the little creek. It was fed by the melting of the snow in the spring and welcomed the ducks and egrets to our campus. In the autumn, under a roof of red leaves, I walked the trail to the river and stood on the rocks near Little Niagara, where the waters of the creek, sparkling and singing, flowed into the Chippewa River and traveled their long journey to the sea by joining the Mighty Mississippi near Durand, Wisconsin.

I had my places to recharge on campus. This enabled me to come back to my office refreshed and better able to listen to and understand people, hopefully bringing laughter and some perspective to the conversations. One of these places for me was the simple, peaceful, and strikingly beautiful University Newman Center chapel, where the gifted music students practice liturgical songs. I could scoot over there for Mass when the campus carillon bells rang out at noon, even though Cindy Leprechaun-Whisperer would tease me about trying to be a "good girl" when I did it. I could drop in there on Ash Wednesday for the (standing room only) ecumenical Passion Play the students put on and get the cross of ashes on my forehead, or go any time to meditate and pray in a quiet, contemplative space.

"I often enjoyed tearful hugs from students at graduation and cozy times of hospitality in my colleagues' offices."

Anyway, Gabriella wrote in her evaluation that I was the professor "who kept her from pulling her hair out." When she would flip into blame and fighting mode, she would come into my office, look out my picture window into the woods, and pour out her frustrations. After a little herbal tea and a listening ear, and maybe some words of empathy, she would get back to herself—her peaceful self. I may have said some words to give her perspective from my forgiveness and health research or the positive psychology unit I had written for the psych nursing class, or I may have just been a centering place for her to regain composure—I don't know.

On the outside of my office door were three small posters: a quote on gratitude from the famous happiness scholar Dr. Sonya Lyubomirsky, a quote from the Buddhist monk Thich Nhat Hanh on mindfully drinking tea, and a diagram of the physiology of laughter. In this quirky, homey place, I tried to help people feel at home, cared for, and respected, and in return, I often enjoyed tearful hugs from students at graduation and cozy times of hospitality in my colleagues' offices.

Many professors' offices brought unique, homey places of refuge to the nursing students. Often, the tiny peach-colored office of a colleague would have eight students jammed in among the plants and sunshine to discuss mentoring other students. Another colleague would have so many students that she was assisting in preparing for the psych exam that students would be sitting on the floor in the hallway overflowing from her office. Another colleague had a couch with a box of Kleenex for distressed students to pour out their troubles in her handkerchief-sized office with a picture window. Each of these professors was to me like a different kind of flower blooming in the school of nursing.

One of the things that made the College of Nursing so welcoming was the pluralism. There was an atmosphere that was mostly light and easy, with an absence of walking on eggshells about our different religions or identities. There was a relaxed sense of openness and, well, *home* in those halls and offices.

For example, a colleague in the peach-colored office next to mine, who immigrated from China and used to chat with me about Buddhist philosophy and Eastern medicine, asked me to speak in one of her classes on the research regarding the effect of praying with patients. So, I took some time to do the literature search to give a lecture about the quantitative studies demonstrating the effect of prayer. My lecture on prayer was filmed, and it was reused for many semesters so that undergrad students in future years recognized me in the hall as the prayer research teacher (to my surprise since it was a tiny slice of what I taught).

To add to the modeling of pluralism to our students, we were lucky enough to have a few male nursing professors in our sea of estrogen (the daughters of Florence Nightingale). One was a young nursing professor who taught Statistics and Men's Health. His children, who sometimes hung out in his office, added to the homey feeling of our college. He told me he was part of a roundtable group that met at his Mosque that included a representative from every religion and atheism, too. The goal was to build respect and a cooperative community. He was a model of acceptance and respect for diversity in our nursing building.

Before "inclusivity" and "pluralism" were key goals campus-wide, our diverse team of nursing faculty tried to model *hospitality to all* and carefully weave into our classes what we called "cultural competence." This helped students of all perspectives feel welcomed and taught them to bring this understanding to the vulnerable people in hospital beds and in clinic rooms. We tried to teach these young, eager nursing students to build connections rather than criticize the "other" people who may passionately hold ideologies or identities differing from our own. We tried to teach not just the science of nursing but the art and heart part, too. To all the pathophysiology and clinical skills, we were happy to add a cup of love and hospitality. Everyday life, either in or out of our homes, can feel richer and more interesting when I value and learn from people who are different than me.

Home Again Moment

"I had my places to recharge on campus." Think of places or practices that help renew and recharge you amid the whirl of responsibilities at home or on the job. Pick one of these places or practices and think of one time it helped you renew yourself. Relive it in your imagination. Savor the memory.

Home Again Questions

What stood out, struck you, or moved you in this chapter?

The staff at the School of Nursing was very diverse, but we had positive *synergy*—one of those words that sounds like "energy" and means that our combined effect was greater than the sum of our separate effects. That is pluralism at its best. Who is a person in your life who is very different from you—maybe very, very different? What is one way that, together, you have a positive effect on your world greater than either of you have separately? Or, reflect on how being with this person adds something to your life, makes a positive difference for you, or helps you to be a better person.

For Further Reflection

What does "pluralism" mean to you? How can you make it a deeper part of your interactions with, and thoughts about, others?

6

Homemaking in My Barstow Street Private Practice

A little clinical office on South Barstow Street in Eau Claire, Wisconsin, became a home where I could endeavor to help people make the foundations for *their* homes.

In 2005, when I was a Nurse Practitioner student at the University of Wisconsin–Eau Claire, I first entered the cozy waiting room and the sunny Barstow Street office of my preceptor Tina. She was a Clinical Nurse specializing in Psychiatry. As I sat in on her sessions with her clients, I was shaken by the brokenness of the homes and families of the people who shared their pain with us. The people who came to share their stories in Tina's office were mostly ordinary Wisconsin teenagers and parents, and husbands and wives whose homes had become so painful that they needed help with their broken hearts, broken communication, and, yes, broken homes. They told stories of romantic betrayal, broken promises, deep hurts, and crushing wounds.

Since much of my graduate school scholarship was on mindfulness practices and forgiveness interventions, Tina gave me the other office and referred seven patients a week to me who needed these approaches. So I tried out my ivory tower knowledge of research on wounded people from wounding homes and had the privilege of witnessing amazing healing of hearts, communication, and homes. After I graduated, I joined Tina in that little office, and even today, when I walk by that place on Barstow Street and look up at the large window of my former office, I am touched and amazed at the miracles that happened in the lives and homes of those precious people that came to me so broken. Here is a little peek into my office in 2006:

"Well yeah . . . but where do I get the power?" Dominic complained sharply to me. He was a tall, dark, and handsome young man in his early 30s. Staring at a picture I had drawn of how the forgiveness process works, the expression on his face said, "Duh!" He got it. He wanted it. The pain in his life from his anger that started at age 13 when his parents divorced was no longer serving him. His parents' response to his anger was empathy and trying to make up for the disruption, but his bosses just fired him when his habitual angry temperament flared, and his fiancé had just dumped him after another fit of anger. How would he make a living or have a family of his own if he couldn't figure out how to find the power to forgive?

"Forgiveness became the foundation of their renewed relationship."

Just to let you know, I did not know the answer to his question, "Where do people get the power to forgive?" It wasn't in the academic ivory tower literature. So I asked him, "Where do *you* get *your* power?"

He paused and thought for a long minute in my sunny office. Then he ventured a guess, "There is an older man from my church. He seems very forgiving. I think I can ask him to talk to me every day on the phone and help me to learn to forgive."

When he came back to my office in a week, he reported, "We decided to memorize the same quote every day about forgiveness and talk to each other on the phone about it."

A few weeks later, I got an unexpected phone call from Keisha, Dominic's ex-fiancé. She said, "I don't know what happened to him, but I want some. I don't have anyone to forgive except myself. I can't forgive myself. Can I come to see you?"

True story: Half a year later, I opened a fancy envelope in my mail and read, "You are invited to the wedding of Dominic and Keisha . . . " Forgiveness became the foundation of their renewed relationship.

I'm not saying that their married life was all French pastries and balloons, but their forgiveness work was a cornerstone to build on. This little clinical office on Barstow Street, with its old furniture, big sunny window, and impressionistic paintings, was a home where I was able to support people who were trying to make or remake a foundation for *their* homes. In that office on Barstow Street, people told of terrible hurts and found healing.

Naturally, I began to look for the answer to Dominic's question, "Where do people get the power to forgive?" Two research projects later, working with a close-knit team of student and faculty researchers, as well as a life coach, we found answers to Dominic's question. These answers came through interviews with *inspiring* people who had forgiven. Some came from homes in which a parent had murdered the other parent, or where there was intimate partner violence, or someone was dying with unresolved broken relationships, or someone was trying to recover from being tortured in war. We distilled what we learned into 12 short, powerful "Guideposts to Forgiveness." They have already helped many people struggling to forgive. You can see them in the *Forgiveness Handout* at the end of the book and use them to help heal your home or the homes of people you care about.

Home Again Moment

How even my office turned into a "home" shows that any place where people feel listened to and cared for can feel like "home." The Guideposts to Forgiveness in *Forgiveness Handout* are not something we made up. They come from interviews with diverse people who have forgiven very difficult wounds. They reveal discoveries from real people about releasing pain and finding peace again after such wounds. Maybe they can be of use to you too, or to someone you love.

Home Again Questions

What stood out, struck you, or moved you in this chapter?

Read the Guideposts in *Forgiveness Handout*. Which one or two of them resonate with you and why?

How can you apply one or two Guideposts to bring more peace to your life or the life of the place you call "home?"

For Further Reflection

Choose a person in your home, family, or life who has caused you trouble. Not the most difficult person you have dealt with, but someone you have struggled with that you want to practice forgiving.

Now, choose a person in your life or in history who

has been an example to you of forgiveness. Imagine that you are with this loving person. Think about how that person treats you. Then, in your imagination, together with this person who is an example to you of forgiveness, gently look at the person who has caused you trouble. Give yourself a few moments. What unfolds?

7

Comfort and Joy
on the East Hill

I had totally figured out swearing rules. Swearing fell into three categories in our home in the 1950s and '60s. Dignified swearing that only grown men got away with. Even though now Germany and Japan are beloved allies, in the '50s, I would overhear "Those damn Japs and Germans" grunted by the dads huddled in the neighborhood, smoking Lucky Strikes and swapping war stories. The exception is that kids in the family could sing (for company) a song my dad wrote in the war that ends with him kissing someone in his dream and telling her, "That this bloody war is hell."

Then, there was merry swearing, like my mom saying "the whole fam-damn-ily" or hauling us girls out to sing in harmony for guests a song written in 1916 about Patrick Clancy, the painter man, misspelling Timothy Kelly's name on a sign. The song goes, "If I knock the 'L' out of KELLY, it would still be KELLY to me, for a single 'LY' or a double 'LY' would look just the same to an Irishman's eyes . . . but if I knock the 'L' out of KELLY, he will knock the 'L' out of me."

All other swearing fell into the category of dirty swearing and could get my mouth washed out with soap. However, this rule lost all its teeth when my parents had grandchildren. My mom's laughter at being corrected by a toddler confirmed the rule had become obsolete. "No, Grandma, it's not son of a gun, it's son of a b***h."

"These handsome parents of ours, in the photos on the wall, passed on their artistry. . . . They also gave us a heritage of laughter."

So anyway, 2022 has been the kind of winter that makes people want to swear on the East Hill of Eau Claire, Wisconsin, and it's still fall by the calendar (only December 6). The sidewalks and roads are skating rinks that we are fighting with salt and sand. Stumbling out of COVID, not wearing masks, the middle school is full of respiratory illness and flu. In our multigenerational household, our grandchild is either home sick with a fever and cough or slow-bloodedly taking the bus in the dark and cold, struggling with all the make-up work. Our son is jogging in homemade cleated sneakers on the ice, driving on the icy roads to the store for sick day foods for his son, helping a friend who is out of work recovering from shoulder surgery after falling on the ice, or staying up late to catch up on work.

Our heating prices have soared, and everything from frozen chicken breasts to car repairs costs more. Putin's threats are disturbing our hearts here. I worry. I struggle to cheer myself up. Our usually upbeat priest told me he has six funerals to prepare for. One is today, even though the snow on the street in front of our house that goes to the cemetery hasn't been plowed yet. No one knows why there is an excess of death in 2022. And then I think about the merriment I felt last summer when the livin' was easier. And I wonder. Am I only resilient in fair weather? Can I live the comfort and joy of summer in the winter of 2022?

☼☼☼

At about 3:30 on many summer afternoons, someone in our multigenerational household announces, "Surf's Up!" This is an invitation to a family tradition of swimming and usually to talk nonsense while swimming. In the '60s, our family's staycation was swimming from morning until the pool lights went off at the Swim Club. After my mother died, we took the proceeds of her condo and put a swim spa in our backyard in her honor, which we use nine months out of the year.

As we splash around in the jet streams or sit in the water massage seats, we often play a storytelling game with tales of our grandchild's cat. Though the cuddly gray tabby's real-life excitement was catching mice and playing with catnip toys, our stories told of her nine lives when she turns into a superhero or supervillain. (This cat has lived through many harrowing adventures in the space-time continuum, appearing in various historical and futuristic scenarios through eons.) When someone says the word "blue," they must end their turn and let the next person take over the storyline no matter where it goes. After that, it's the game, "Would you rather?"

Like, "Would you rather eat nothing but bananas for a week *or* drink out of the birdbath?"

"How much would I have to drink from the birdbath?"

"Umm, a tablespoon."

Smiling grandchild says, "The birdbath," as if that choice was just a cinch.

I crinkled up my nose, shook my head back and forth, and said, "Eww!"

"Well, it is better than getting hyper-potassium from too many bananas."

Then, our grandchild stumps us with a guessing game as we continue to swim around.

"I'm thinking of something."

"Is it on Earth? Is it food?"

It usually ends satisfactorily with something very elusive, like a proton.

Our five school-age grandchildren invented taking turns being pushed by the spa current towards Grandpa at the opposite end while everyone yelled loud enough to alert the neighbors, "Ten, nine, eight, seven, six, five, four, three, two, one, Grandpa!"

In the evening, when my son and my grandchild put another Asian or Mediterranean meal on the table, there is either silence because the food is too good to talk or nonsensical conversations. Conversations about choice of superpowers or repeating funny lines from movies and TV shows, like *Get Smart*, are woven into the chatter.

After dinner, there is dancing in the kitchen while we do dishes. Inspired by the talk at UW-Superior by the famous health researcher Dr. Kelly McGonigal, we sway, bounce, keep the beat, show off, and demonstrate the "anything goes" style of dancing to tunes we shout out to Alexa. "Happy" (from *Despicable Me 2*), "Walk Like an Egyptian," and "Walking on Sunshine" are kitchen favorites. And our son's favorite: anything by "Weird Al" Yankovic.

After the kitchen is set to rights, we often go to the "room of the Great-Grandparents" in the basement, also known as the entertainment center. Here, we enjoy *Get Smart, Ms. Marvel,* or *Gravity Falls*. It is called the "room of the Great-Grandparents" because the walls are covered with mostly black and white photos taken in the '40s and '50s of our benevolent parents—looking like movie stars dressed in military or formal attire. Besides the swimming tradition passed on by my back-flipping father and my U of I 1950s Dolphin Queen mother (who decorated the Christmas tree with swim team ribbons), we got lots of merry traditions from the wonderful people looking down on us from the picture frames.

Our son's nickname in his high school yearbook, Disco-Dave, and our daughter's ballroom dance talent—they came by these honestly. My parents had season tickets to Lincoln Center in New York to enjoy the ballet and loved to take us to see the dancers at Broadway musicals. In the '70s in Madison, Wisconsin, Dad would put a big band record on the turntable in our family room and teach each of his teenage daughters which beat was a waltz and which beat was a polka, even if we stepped on his feet. "One-two-three. Hear it? You will need to know this when you go to weddings."

These handsome parents of ours, in the photos on the wall, passed on their artistry. Our home has been graced with my father-in-law's still-life paintings, stained glass masterpieces, quirky creations like lamps made from a fire extinguisher and a parking meter, and a table made from an industrial wire spool. We cuddle up in my husband's stepmom's crocheted blankets.

They also gave us a heritage of laughter. Lou's mom was a Chicago waitress who laughed at his dad's jokes so much that it led to a happy marriage (even though it was unfortunately short because she died of cancer). His dad knew just how to poke fun and get shy toddlers giggling on his lap.

Lou's dad and mom.

Our grandchildren's
great-grandparents: Lou's dad
and step-mom.

People still groan at my dad's "dad" jokes, like saying, "People are dying to get in there" *every* time we pass a cemetery. My mom's Danbury, Connecticut, Women's Club friends said the best part of a meeting was when my mom would take the microphone. She shocked people into gasping laughter by just being unexpectedly honest. Once, a buff woman in UW–Madison's Women's Club suggested Mom shouldn't join the tennis club because "We play really hard tennis." My mom deadpanned, "I don't recommend you join the book club because we read really dirty books." She was just being honest. The shock of vulgar, dirty swearing in most of the book club choices in the '60s made them really hard for her to read.

The reunion in heaven of my parents with my kids will be merry. The deaths of my father and mother were very hard. I have never gotten used to death, even though I was the Mayo nurse who was called to the bedside to help patients and families adjust to starting hospice, and later served as a bedside chaplain at St. Joseph's Hospital in Chippewa Falls.

When my first patient died at Madison Convalescent Center, I physically shook with a sense of failure as I stood in the cramped nurse's station in my white dress, polished white shoes, white stockings, and white cap. I was trying to figure out who to assign to wash the body, composing myself to phone her family, and continuing to medicate and change bandages for the other 20 patients under my care. I was hardly able to comfort anyone because I was so much in need of comfort myself. I felt I had failed to keep this person alive.

I was only prepared at college to save lives, but I learned to comfort and help people with the inevitable transition of mortality on my weekend shifts. At the Scandinavian Lutheran Nursing Home, I worked at in Eau Claire in the '90s, most people died on the weekend after their loved ones came to say goodbye. I ordered food trays for the families and told staff to report any signs of the patient's discomfort. Many of my dying patients have told me of the joy of seeing their deceased relatives or Jesus or having poignant epiphanies about the meaning of life. As someone who taught assessing and prescribing for dementia to doctoral students, I do *not* dismiss these dreams and visions full of comfort as confusion.

The joyful mystery of connection with multigenerational family members in heaven feels like a relay race in which the baton is passed from generation to generation. These merry people in heaven are still part of our intergenerational family.

Even in our dark winter of 2022, my son picks up this baton of merriment when he plays "Duck Chess" with his son, or they sing about greasy corn while getting out the knives, frying pans, and Chinese wine to make "Chinese" venison stir fry. (Thank you, Aleks and your northern Wisconsin relatives, for bagging so many deer.) For the record, Duck Chess involves detailed negotiations of new rules of chess that govern everything two little pawn-sized ceramic ducks (that came in a sushi set) can do.

It's been a good winter so far on the Eastside Hill. We've been working together on shoveling, making Christmas surprises, and girding ourselves with merriment for the long winter since it is still fall. Bring it on! Comfort and Joy! Snow forts, blowing bubbles that freeze before they pop, hot chocolate by the fire, snowmen, and snow days with no school!

Home Again Moment

Gratitude is a great protection in life from being overwhelmed by discouragement and hopelessness.

The University of Pennsylvania, the home of Martin Seligman, known as the Father of Positive Psychology, has a website on Happiness Research. That is where I learned of the gratitude exercises that go head to head in research with antidepressants in restoring happiness. One of the exercises is to write down every week (or every night) a list of a few things you savor and are grateful for. In a tiny spiral notebook by my bed, I often just write the date and five words that represent memories of the day to treasure before I fall asleep. For example: "Salmon, Phone Call, Song, Sunshine, God."

Home Again Questions

What stood out, struck you, or moved you in this chapter?

What are you grateful for? What are five things in the last day or the last week you can savor and put on your gratitude list?

When you are having a hard time, what are practical ways you can remind yourself to be more aware of things in your routine or people in your life that bring you comfort or joy?

For Further Reflection

Remembering special people in our lives today and in the past can give us comfort and joy, especially when we are going through a hard time. It can also inspire us to bring comfort and joy to others. What is one way this week you can plan to give comfort and joy to someone in your life?

8

The DNA of Loyalty to Our Home Team

As soon as we parked our four bikes by the shining lake full of ducks, we heard the sounds rolling down the hill from Upper Carson Park's football stadium to our picnic table at Lower Carson Park. The sounds were from the band playing at the University of Wisconsin–Eau Claire's opening season home game. We came for the music. We fed the ducks bits of our sub sandwiches at Half Moon Lake as we listened. We could hear the announcer, the roar of the crowd when a player ran into the end zone, and most importantly, the band since our grandchild was just starting marching band in school. Our family watched (via our phones) the Eau Claire Blugold football team fight for victory over Decorah, Iowa's Luther College Norse team.

We cheered hard. Our grandchild was so happy that our Eau Claire home team creamed the boys in white and blue from Luther College because, as a Wisconsinite, he had heard and told a lot of Iowa jokes.

"What do the bottoms of Coke bottles say in Iowa?"

"Open other end."

Wisconsin is considered a purple state of polarized blue (liberal Democrats) and red (conservative Republicans), but we *all* fly Green Bay Packers and UW–Madison Badger flags.

I grew up singing the University of Illinois fight song and tailgating with my parents during football season. My mother was the U of I homecoming queen in 1949. We wore her crown with the big "I" on it when we played dress-up, and we felt like we owned that football stadium. But that team loyalty does not compare to the warmth of Wisconsin's loyalty to its beloved Packers. My next-door neighbor owns a share in the Packers, along with half a million other individual Packer fans. No one is allowed to have more than 4 percent of the shares because they are not a corporate team. They belong to Wisconsin folks.

Our neighbor, Harry, makes pilgrimages to Lambeau Field in Green Bay, Wisconsin, to sit outside in the subzero weather with Wisconsinites wearing cheesehead hats. People joke that toddlers can play outside on the streets during Packer games because there is no traffic. East Hill neighbors who fill their yards with Republican signs and neighbors who bring lunch to the Democratic headquarters to feed the canvassers, both say, "How 'bout them Packers, hey?" Even the Amish men in Eau Claire County, who are not supposed to pick up the ways of the modern farmers (like electricity and gas engines), sneak over to their "English" (AKA non-Amish) friends' houses for Packer games.

We Wisconsinites also love our Badgers and sing, "If you want to be a Badger, just come along with me." My dad, who even looked dignified when we sat together at boisterous UW Badger Basketball games in Madison, Wisconsin, would tell me, "It is important to be here because it connects us with history and is part of history in the making."

We love to root for our neighborhood teams. When Dad would buy me a bratwurst topped with hot mustard on a bun at Vilas Park in Madison while we rooted for a local baseball team, he explained, "This is part of being a Wisconsinite: loyalty to your home team."

This team loyalty doesn't just apply to our sports teams but to our schools, our favorite bars, and our churches. It is essential to our feeling of being at home.

Now, here is a true turn-of-the-century Eau Claire story. I heard it from the pulpit by a local priest at St. Patrick's. The names have been changed. Let's just say one of the Kelly sisters, who attended St. Patrick's, wanted to marry a handsome young man who attended the ornate church built by German-speaking families high on the hill on the near north side of Eau Claire. Her father appealed to her loyalty and spoke in his Irish brogue, "You have to marry someone from your own religion." The poor girl went for a second opinion to Father Campbell (real name), the pastor of her family's Catholic Church, St. Patrick's, on the near west side of Eau Claire. The priest appealed to the father to let his daughter marry the young man because the young man's church, Sacred Heart of Eau Claire, was Catholic, too. Come to find out that those down-to-earth west-side sons of Ireland and those proper north-side Germans were on the same team! Now, the congregations in the two parishes have a good laugh at the forbidden marriage story because they are all part of the same parish and share a priest.

This is a story of how, one summer, I was a stranger in a strange land. Yet I discovered how a person whose life was so different than mine could make me feel at *home*. How someone who wasn't my gender, my race, or in my economic circumstances could make me feel so connected, and how we discovered we were kindred spirits on the same home team.

In 2016, my summer class at Case Western University ended early in order for me to be able to safely fly out of Cleveland, and so the local nurses taking the class could take extra shifts to staff the ERs. They were expecting heavy injuries from impending riots. The Republican convention was coming to a place of extreme polarization and historic race riots. I discovered that Cleveland is a divided city that can be summed up in one word: inequality. When I was in Cleveland that summer to get a post-master in geriatrics, I stayed in a hotel that was full of people who were patients or new staff at the nearby world-famous Cleveland Clinic. The clinic was expanding and hiring the best in the world for high salaries. The staff of the hotel, who received tips for parking cars and cleaning, were almost all local African American people. Their minimum wage was below 5 dollars an hour, and their tattered shoes and poor dental health did not match their crisp, official hotel uniforms. I felt a strong connection to the friendly African American hotel workers because they were the ones who talked to me and told me their stories while I stayed there alone studying for seven days. One of them gave me a tip on a Greek takeout place nearby.

I made a picnic of my Greek soup one afternoon. On the beautiful nearby campus of Cleveland Clinic, off Carnegie Avenue, I sat on the grass in the warm sun near the hospital. I was wearing wraparound sunglasses to keep the allergens from further puffing up my red eyes, a long tan trench coat, and a navy, draping hat covering my hair and shoulders. It was inappropriate for the weather, but I needed to keep the pollen off me. As soon as I sat down, I spilled my Greek soup down the front of my trench coat!

Next, a 30-something African American man walked over to me and said, "Hello."

I said, "Hi, I was hoping to meet people."

"Then, don't dress like that."

He kindly sat down to talk and asked me where I was from. When I started to talk about Wisconsin, he said, "I thought you were a homeless person like me."

"You look like you had just been discharged from the nearby psychiatric unit," he said, pointing to the hospital. He was concerned because I looked lost.

He asked me again, "Where are you from?"

"Wisconsin." When I was talking to him about Wisconsin, I must have said something that sounded professorial by accident.

He suddenly turned an angry face to me, raised his voice, and said, "You think you are talking to a dumb black man!" The inequality between us was a gulf that caused his face to flush with hatred.

I started to cry.

Spoiler alert—plot twist.

Startled, he said, "I'm going to have to cheer you back up," and sang a song from the 1950s. He said it was good for "old white ladies." He sang (or should I say performed) for me the song "Young at Heart" with a twinkle in his eye and a voice to rival Frank Sinatra himself. I felt like I was suddenly in a fairy tale. His music made me dry my tears and laugh with delight.

By the end of the song, written to inspire old people to be full of love and young at heart, which he sang with a smile (even more winning than Ol' Blue Eyes), we were friends.

He answered all my nosy questions about what it was like to have no permanent place to live. "Where do you sleep? How do you shower? How do you stay safe? Where do you find strength?"

To the last question, he told me about his inner-city church and sang to me, in tears, a worship song of gratefulness for Jesus dying for his sins. We were already friends. He had me at "hello," but now I knew we were on the same team. We cried at the same song.

He walked me back to my hotel arm in arm as he sang more songs to me, though he was very hesitant because he said, "There are lots of policemen near that hotel." He was afraid they would think he was taking advantage of me.

I said, "No problem. I am good with policemen." Police bias was in favor of an old white lady with a University of Wisconsin staff ID, highlighting another divide between an inner-city African American man and me. A divide we had bridged.

Back at the hotel, I, of course, also felt a connection to my medical colleagues and university scholars who instructed me and rode the elevators with me. What in the world did the people who were barely subsisting and these privileged medical people have in common? How could they even connect with each other to bridge the gap in a way that could rebuild their city and overcome the highest poverty rate in the nation—with about half of their children living with food insecurity? There is no magic bullet for Cleveland, but I do know what those rich and poor people were talking about to each other in the elevators, in the crosswalks, and in the grocery store lines. They were talking about their home team, the Cavaliers. They smiled at each other and said hopeful, joyful words about their team. It was in the DNA of Cleveland, everybody's *home team*, a shared loyalty that made very different people feel at home with one another. And that year, their beloved Cavaliers came from behind to defeat the Golden State Warriors for the championship.

Wisconsinites too, have a shared loyalty that makes it easier to feel at home with each other. They have the Green Bay Packers in their DNA. You can take the Packer fans out of Wisconsin, but you can find a Packer bar in 50 states and all the corners of the globe. In our news, there is a lot about a red-blue civil war coming, akin to Ireland's violent conflict. How do we prevent or cure high conflict? Well, in Colombia, the government started its amazingly successful strategy to de-radicalize a long-standing violent rebel group by airing television advertisements during the Colombian football (soccer) games to appeal to the rebels who would have rather been home watching the game with their mothers than in hiding. Our shared home team can be bigger than our side of the conflict.

Political loyalties have greatly divided our nation. Our church members and neighbors seem to be evenly split on politics (based on yard signs). But my experience here in Eau Claire is that we have managed to care deeply about people with whom we do not always see eye to eye. To me, our community feels like a home team. Our loyalty to each other in our neighborhoods, schools, and churches, for the most part, is bigger than political loyalty. Why? I believe it is because we are connected to our community's histories—and our memories.

When I am dumping through a gray December day, I remember things that connect me to my community, like learning to dance the "Packerina" at my neighbor's house. Or I laugh remembering when, during one of the Packers' Super Bowls, my neighbor, JulieAnn, said to her husband, Gunnar, "Here comes Ann crossing the street in her pajamas." Everyone was wearing green and gold swag, and my only appropriate outfit was my Packer pajamas. I feel a deep sense of the history that connects me to my fellow Wisconsinites, no matter their politics, when I remember the feeling of singing the regal Wisconsin century-old song, "Varsity! Varsity! U-rah-rah! Wisconsin!"

The memory of singing joyfully together with my Eau Claire neighbors as we lit candles outside of Immaculate Conception Church on Easter Eve and processioned into the dark church together gives me a deep sense of being on the same team in spite of differing political loyalties. (Catholics are a mixture of blue Democrats and red Republicans.)

"Wisconsinites too, have a shared loyalty that makes it easier to feel at home with each other."

All over Eau Claire, Easter is celebrated in the old churches given to us by very diverse people. I sense the history that unites Eau Claire when I think of all the different families that put their heart and soul into leaving us the heritage of beautiful churches. The Irish immigrants who built sturdy St. Patrick's, the Germans who built the ornate Sacred Heart on the hill, and the young Scandinavian families who built the beautiful Lutheran churches. Not to mention the people of English heritage who built the august Episcopal Cathedral on the corner of Lake and Farwell downtown, where they welcomed the Greek immigrants to use the church for services and diverse young people for dances in the spacious Great Hall. The ability of these founders of Eau Claire to become a united community in spite of coming from various places around the globe, various political parties, and different levels of affluence is part of my history. Part of *our* history. Part of our DNA.

Home Again Moment

When people are very different from us in their perspectives, lifestyle, or religion, we can fall into dehumanizing them or at least disassociating with them, and failing to feel that dialogue is possible. The solution is empathy and a connection to our common humanity—finding ways to see we are on the same team.

Home Again Questions

What stood out, struck you, or moved you in this chapter?

Is there anyone that is hard to see as being on your team, or see as your neighbor? Someone with a different political or moral take on things? Someone with a different standard of cleanliness or different abilities? What are ways you can see them, in their humanness, as on the same team as you are?

For Further Reflection

We can try to go beyond winning or losing in a disagreement with someone at home or with a friend and just aim to build understanding. When conversing with someone you don't agree with, have you ever tried *paraphrasing* back to the person (with respect and empathy) what you think you heard them say and checking to see if you understood? Sometimes, that is called *the empathy loop*. If you do a web search for "Harvard and empathy loop," you'll find some interesting stuff.

9

Slow Home: Our Scandinavian Roots

Last night, my husband and I went on a relaxing date, the first one we had enjoyed since the COVID pandemic began. On our way to the theater, we strolled down historic Barstow Street in Eau Claire, Wisconsin, on a crisp, early spring evening, taking time to soak in the beauty of downtown with all the trees that line each side of the street wrapped in white lights. We sat in the balcony, laughed, and clapped as we watched the world premiere of a radio drama parody, *Sam Shovel, Private Eye*. Sam, a trench coat-clad 1940s gal with a brunette bob showing out of her fedora hat, solves the kidnapping of a Pekingese dog. It is full of action, adventure, and puns, just like the real life of the playwrights: a couple who live in Eau Claire, the quirky Jim and Jane Jeffries. When they are not writing plays, they take care of grandchildren or a parent, teach, or run off to Europe. But in all the busyness of the Jeffries' lives, they also know how to *slow down*.

Sitting around the Jeffries' dining table, surrounded by friends on a deep and quiet winter Sunday evening, Jim (the comic writer) burst into song as we ate rice and African greens. We were discussing possible names for what was turning into a close-knit dinner and prayer group. It was a little oasis of "Island Time," that leisurely pace of the Pacific Islands *and* the upper Midwest on Sunday nights. We talk about our week and mostly take the time to listen to each other. When we came up with the name "Feeling Groovy Group," Jim Jeffries sang "The 59th Street Bridge Song (Feelin' Groovy)" by Simon and Garfunkel, recommending us to slow down in order to feel groovy.

Slowing down has become a global movement ever since thousands of enraged Italians, organized by Carlo Petrini, filled the Piazza di Spagna in 1986 to protest against McDonald's opening its doors and corrupting their culture of farm-to-table cuisine with corporate fast food. Cultural rebellion against the pace of life being too fast to meet universal needs for creativity, play, happiness, savoring, and health has led to the Slow Movement. It was organized around Slow Art, Slow Cinema, Slow Aging, Slow Parenting, Slow Gaming, Slow Gardening, Slow Cities, and just plain Slow Living on a Slow Planet.

☼☼☼

In my 30s, I greeted a beautiful brunette middle-aged woman in a busy bathroom at New York's LaGuardia Airport.

She burst into tears and said, "Where are you from?"

I said, "Wisconsin."

"I'm from Wisconsin, too! No one has ever taken the time to greet me in a women's public bathroom since my father dropped me off a decade ago in New York City to take a job singing in the Metropolitan Opera."

She treated me to a leisurely lunch as I waited for my plane to take me from my slow place, Eau Claire, Wisconsin, to another slow place, New London, New Hampshire.

☼☼☼

Eau Claire is a town slow enough to notice the sun moving across the sky and a car driving by the front porch. I met a family that told me they moved to Eau Claire—the upper Midwest Sea of Lutherans and Catholics by lakes and rivers in farmland—because of listening to a public radio drama, "The News from Lake Wobegon," depicting our pace of life. They wanted in.

Our hometown's pace is rooted in the undeniable fact that the city is awash with Scandinavians. I have met few Eau Claire natives who are ignorant of the meaning of the Danish word hygge (pronounced hooga): the prototype of slow, protected, cozy living dating to Old Norse traditions in the Middle Ages. Eau Claire, founded by New England financiers of the lumber industry in the 1800s, soon attracted Scandinavian loggers and artisans, who felt at home in the snow.

As I walk near the confluence of the Eau Claire and Chippewa Rivers in downtown Eau Claire, I can see evidence of the prominence of Norse culture in the 1930s at 204 East Grand. The beautiful brick building still bears a plaque near the entrance that reads, "Scandinavian American Fraternity Building." Yes, and I still hear people saying "Uff-da" when they get bad news, and talking with the musicality of the Northwoods dialect that sounds a little like English with a Swedish accent. Nursing homes serve Lutefisk and Lefse. (I am surprised Lutefisk is legal, considering it is old fish soaked in lye for months! Lefse, a thinly rolled potato crepe, is good with butter and cinnamon sugar.) Half the names in the White Pages end with "son" (like "Johnson") or "sen" because their ancestors were the sons and daughters of Lars, John, Sever, and Ander. Refrigerator magnets around town say things like, "You can always tell a Swede, but you can't tell him much."

Hygge is a cultural concept where things aren't necessarily done at a snail's pace but at the right pace to still savor life. It's about taking time, out of the rush of life, to be together with people you care about—slowing down enough so you have time to sit around in wool socks—while toasting your toes by the fire with friends and drinking hot cocoa or mulled wine. Hygge, for me, is enjoying a card game of Kings in a Corner or Chess with a grandkid or playing Croquet in a local park with a local Croquet champion like Allen Perkins. Hygge is spontaneously welcoming our neighbor, Josh Gallagher, into our living room and listening to him make our 100-year-old upright piano resonate with the sound of improvised jazz worthy of a stage at New York's Lincoln Center.

"Hygge, koselig, and lagom in our homes require a resting heart."

We just put in a new wood stove in our living room this week, and I spent the entire morning yesterday tending a fire to be at the exact temperature to cure the woodstove's paint. I loved the feel and smell of the kindling and the split oak as I loaded the firebox, and the beauty of the calm crackling fire of the slow-burning logs through the glass.

As an awestruck 10-year-old, I gazed at the first fireplace I ever saw. I was in Canada on a trip to a cabin with my parents and siblings. Eating blueberries we had just picked and reminiscing about seeing a mother bear and her cubs on Blueberry Hill, we stared into the fireplace, fascinated by the flames and sparks. My dad said, "A fool will stare at a wall, but a wise man can sit for hours gazing at a fire."

In my hometown, there is time to gaze into fires, sit in a sauna, ice fish, and snowshoe in the winter. We walk down our block to Seven Bump Hill, where we can slide even if we don't bring a sled because there is a sled lending library. In Eau Claire, if you don't have snowshoes, poles, an ice fishing rod, a sledding helmet, or sleds—no problem, there is free winter-gear-share all over the area. And, of course, there are many free groomed ice rinks for games, figure skating, and hockey. In the summer, there is time to swim in Big Falls (a nearby waterfall), gaze at the sparkles on Half Moon Lake, lie on the beaches, and tube or boat down the Chippewa and Eau Claire Rivers and feel groovy.

The Norwegians who settled in Eau Claire brought the concept of "koslig." It is like hygge but adds the idea of taking time to savor life out in nature. The long winter gives us time to appreciate uniquely Northwoods nature while walking or fishing on icy lakes and appreciating the bright red Cardinals, Blue Jays, and peaceful Mourning Doves, who like our cold days. When the snow melts, the wonder of the Robins returning and the blackberries ripening in the neighborhood woods feels almost miraculous.

Don't get me wrong, Upper Midwesterners are famous for their productivity. My brassy blond corporate nurse manager, who also taught part-time at the tech college, drove a bright orange sports car, partied hard (while raising five kids who she taught to go to church *and* have fun), used to sign all her emails, "Have a productive day!" I wish I had a nickel for every time I hear a story of someone being hired in another state because of one word on their application. The word was "Wisconsin." But the Swedes who settled in many of the bungalows on the East Hill brought more than the Midwest productivity ethic. They brought to our homes the cultural concept of "lagom" to help us decide the balance and speed of our particular life and situation. We don't have an English word to translate "lagom"; it is something like "not too much and not too little." Just right! It's how Goldilocks measured the porridge she ate, the bed she slept in, and the chair she sat on in the bears' house.

☼☼☼

I am grateful to all the dear Swedish, Norwegian, and Danish grandmothers and grandfathers in Eau Claire who gave us a balanced heritage of not only productivity but happiness. These Scandinavian countries knock it out of the park on the World Happiness Index, which measures the culture of countries by a yardstick of six items that go beyond the Gross Domestic Product to include things that *take time*. Things like improving health, helping neighbors, giving people choices, supporting those in need, and ethical decision-making. Of the 150 countries that are polled on the Index, countries that rank the highest year after year include all those Scandinavian countries. Yah, it is not just their Ole and Lena jokes that make them the happiest places on earth.

Hygge, koselig, and lagom in our homes require a resting heart.

Over the years, I have spent many hours in a simulation lab on the second floor of the Nursing building nestled in the woods on the University of Wisconsin–Eau Claire campus. It was full of expensive mannequins in hospital beds and nursing students dressed in crisp white lab coats with brand-new stethoscopes hanging around their necks.

These nervous second-year students put their stethoscopes on the mannequins' chests and listened. Then, I quizzed them on what they heard. In medicine, we measure something called Heart Rate Recovery. A healthy heart can speed up when the body needs to produce lots of energy to run or handle a crisis, and then it recovers at a slow, relaxed resting rate. The heart needs time to fill its chambers and to settle down its muscles between beats. The "lagom" heart rests at least as much as it works, and usually, it rests about twice as long as it works, not too much or too little. The heart of a "lagom" home settles down to just the right amount of slowness to feel groovy.

Here is a groovy Ole and Lena joke, in case you are curious:

So anyway, Ole died in a snowmobile accident.

His wife Lena wrote a beautiful page-long obituary mentioning what a great ice fisherman, Packer fan, and Lutheran Ole was. She also mentioned that he was a wonderful father to Greta, Lars, and Sven.

The newspaper office then let her know that the first five words of the obituary are free, and then it's 10 cents a word. She revised the obituary to read:

"Ole died. Boat for sale."

Home Again Moment

"Hygge" is a cultural concept in which things aren't necessarily done at a snail's pace but at the right pace to savor life.

"Koslig" is like hygge but adds the idea of taking time to savor life out in *nature*.

"Lagom" is something like "not too much and not too little." Just right!

Home Again Questions

What stood out, struck you, or moved you in this chapter?

Which of these concepts resonates with you the most? Why?

If our heart doesn't rest between beats just the right amount, we can have tachycardia (unusually fast heartbeats—which can lead to irregular heart rhythms and even strokes and heart attacks). What helps you to rest just the right amount to have a healthy heart and home?

For Further Reflection

Who are models to you of the pace that gives time to savor life? How can you imitate them?

BEGINNINGS

10

Juggling Homemaking in the Thick of It

My father (second from the left) in his home
under the sea in a submarine during WWII.

"The bank of the soap," replied Saverio Recine to the practical inquiry of his beautiful date. "Which bank is your money in?" my husband's grandmother, Angelina Esposito, asked the man she eventually married. He called it the "bank of the soap" because the money he deposited had been washed away. This was before Roosevelt signed the FDIC law federally insuring money in the banks.

Homemaking in the 1930s was an act of courage. It took courage for Angelina Esposito to marry Saverio Recine when their first date was not going out to eat or to the movies but being a recipient of a piece of gum and taking a walk in their Italian neighborhood in Chicago. It took courage to feed their three children in the city during the Great Depression. But Angelina told me that they managed by having "Pasta Fazool" (noodles and beans) every meal except Sunday. On Sunday, they ate chicken because the children worked all Saturday at a butcher shop in exchange for it.

It took courage for my paternal grandfather, Lee Gentry, to give up a prestigious political career when he was asked to be a Cabinet appointee by President Franklin D. Roosevelt. He chose to stay on as the manager of Sinnissippi Farm, the governor's northern Illinois farm, where he knew his children would have milk, eggs, meat, and vegetables during the Great Depression. He feared he could not make his family's dinner table as plentiful in Washington.

"Homemaking in the 1930s was an act of courage."

It took courage for my mother's mother, Thelma Wilbourn, to kill Mom's pet rooster to feed her five girls some fried chicken on a special picnic, even though my mom cried. Thelma was a single, working mom because her husband had died. She managed to make their little white house in Olive Branch, Illinois, a heavenly place in sickness, health, life, and death through prayer, courage, and ingenuity while working in a social work job for the state of Illinois and running the family peach orchard. She raised five girls who were devout Catholics their whole lives and who gave her 17 grandchildren. She worked hard to keep her children fed and clothed and taught them the importance of every woman having an education in case there arose a need to be a provider.

My grandma understood the helplessness of impoverished women through her work in social services. When I was 7, I rode with her in her old car on a dusty road on her visit to a poor rural family. The family lived in a shack. This opened my eyes to the need for women to be prepared and courageous in protecting their families. I stayed in the car but was shocked when a little girl my age and a younger child wandered out of the house to look at me. They were filthy and almost naked. I asked my grandmother lots of questions about what I saw as we drove along. I saw my grandmother's grit on that car ride and understood how hard she had worked to bring up my mother and her sisters during the 1930s.

I admit to having a fascination with homemaking in 1930s and '40s Europe during World War II. On my way to junior high, as I bounded out of my backyard down the steep, wooded shoulder of Mount Pisgah in Winchester, Massachusetts, I sang aloud, imagining that I was Maria in the opening scene of *The Sound of Music*. (You know, the scene where Julie Andrews is on the mountain singing about the hills being alive!) I bonded with this movie, which was then in the theater, and listened to the record over and over in our living room, imagining that I was living in the 1930s.

Our next-door neighbors on the East Hill of Eau Claire, who have done many movie nights with us, know that anything with Nazis and nuns will be a hit with me. The courageous, singing, sewing ex-nun making a house into a home for the Von Trapp family during a Nazi invasion taught me about homemaking in the thick of it.

I helped write a study guide for *Number the Stars*, a children's book about the ordinary people who bravely welcomed Jewish families into their homes in Scandinavia during the war. I learned so much about the people in Europe who fed, clothed, and comforted the Jewish people they hid from the Nazis. They also fed the pets, freshened up the curtains, and dusted the furniture, waiting in hope for the return of their Jewish neighbors from concentration camps. When the trains brought back surviving Scandinavian Jews at the end of the war, the people threw flowers at the passing trains on their way home. When the Danish government was asked to give statistics of how many Jews they saved during the war, they responded that Danes do not distinguish between Jews and non-Jews. My preeminent guide to homemaking in the thick of it during the war is Miep Gies.

She was an ordinary Dutch woman who had an asteroid between Mars and Jupiter named after her in 1972. She was the woman who, for almost 3 years, made the Secret Annex, the hiding place of Anne Frank's family in Amsterdam, into a home. She helped make a small living space on the second and third floor of Otto Frank's business at Prinsengracht 263 in Amsterdam, a little more comfortable with creative sacrifices of her war rations and her clandestine trips behind the secret bookcase entrance after business hours. She not only brought them food but also baked cakes and made poems and presents for special occasions. She gave them a listening ear and even spent the night with them at times to bring a little fun into the Secret Annex.

After the war, Otto Frank, Anne's father, was the only survivor in his family. Even though Otto Frank was rich enough to afford better, he chose to live in a tiny flat with Miep, her husband, and the man who owned the apartment. In the difficult days after the war, when food was scarce and grief was raw, Miep had a knack for making the best of little. She was able to make their home nice and cozy, and she took time to listen to everyone.

Miep was a businesswoman who, before the war, had worked in Otto Frank's spices, herbs, and pectin business. And she had a special gift for creating what the Dutch call "gezellig." Gezellig is a word like the English word "coziness" but also connotes the ideas of sociable, intimate, and snug. She did all this in the thick of it. People in Europe after the war were depleted and had no reserve of energy anymore. And yet there was "gezellig."

All homes can deplete their reserves of energy. Once, I counted nine Christmases in a row when we had the flu in our home. When we were in the COVID "thick of it," I read a book about Miep Gies and was reminded that I didn't need great strength and energy as much as perspective. The 1930s and '40s give me perspective.

A large crucifix on our dining room wall (brought from Italy by Angelina Recine, Lou's grandmother) reminds me of where I want to turn my mind back to when unhappy complaints begin to seep in. It has a secret compartment with old brown paper bearing the names of our ancestors whose hope is full of immortality. It also reveals the names of the elementary schools they hailed from in Naples and Rome. When she was in her 70s, she brought it from her home in an Italian Chicago neighborhood to our little bungalow on the East Hill of Eau Claire, Wisconsin, and pronounced a blessing on our family. Looking at this crucifix gives me perspective when I'm in the thick of it. This crucifix is asking something of me—to make the little sacrifices that I need to make in my attitude to constantly be turning back to home again and again.

Home Again Moment

When I think of the '40s, I am inspired by people like my dad, who was in sick bay in a submarine and used the time to write a song we sang later in our home. I am inspired by the story of the British mother who invited the officer who was coming to tell her that her son was dead in for tea. The officer wondered how she could so kindly make tea for him in this circumstance. She said that her father taught her that when any great tragedy comes, think of what you would have done if it had not come and do that.

Home Again Questions

What stood out, struck you, or moved you in this chapter?

Think of times you have been in the thick of it. Who have been examples to you of how to manage when you are depleted and weak?

What about them inspired you?

For Further Reflection

Think back over your life and think about when you have been "in the thick of it" and still managed to continue to try to bring your gifts or your comfort to others. Journal about that time. Remember it and share it with someone. We all need inspiration.

My Parents' Homemaking When We Were Young

My brother and me when we lived in the
little green house in the '50s.

My mom (Pat) would get us excited about our dad's (Bob's) homecoming from work by having us each take turns making the centerpiece for supper. When it was my brother's turn, he would put his electric train on the table with the controls near his plate so he could run it on the tracks to whoever needed the items it carried. The butter was on the flat car, peas in the coal car, and so on. Sometimes, the centerpiece was an odd arrangement of dandelions and zinnias gathered from the yard. Some days, one of my younger sister's ideas for a centerpiece was a conglomeration of dolls in various stages of undress.

There were six birthday parties a year celebrated in our tiny rectangular green box of a three-bedroom house built in the '40s on a block of other little rectangular houses full of children, animals, and birthday parties. In this little Midwestern haven, my parents raised a family of four kids. My mom taught us to be the welcoming committee when my dad got home from work because he always looked tired from his days of checking revenue intake of state and federal budgets and expenditures of the university on research and faculty. He worked in a cubicle with an adding machine and metal file cabinets at the University of Illinois Champaign-Urbana, and by the time he had carpooled home with the other men on the street, he looked beat.

My cousin, Chris, remembers our home as happy, noisy, and with one kid after another taking a turn on my dad's lap. Children were welcome, and never did I hear that a child should be seen and not heard. Each child was able, as we grew up, to have as many friends over as we wanted. My mom once said about our cramped house, "Everything in this house moves every day." Since we had four children in the family and each had a few friends, our backyard playhouse, sandbox, swing set, picnic table, and inside toy box often were filled with noisy kids. My mom would bring out Kool-Aid, vanilla wafers, and homemade popsicles and fill a baby pool with warmish water for us on the hot summer days of Central Illinois.

For my ninth birthday, my parents gave me a crucifix that hung over my top bunk and a new blue bicycle. One night, my dad saw I was crying when he came to tuck me in and asked why. I said, "Because of what Jesus suffered for me on the cross to take away my sins." He replied, "I think Jesus would want you to be happy about that." Good point, yet for me, they were happy tears.

My dad told me he was a convert to the Catholic Church, and he heard there were a lot of bad Catholics, so he decided that if he became one, he would be serious about his faith. My mom had a little statue of the Blessed Virgin Mary on her dresser, and she told me that she had never once left the faith her mother taught her. She taught us a little prayer before eating. And one for before bed, that included an unlikely phrase to suggest to a highly sensitive, imaginative child (who was already wondering if there were snakes under the bed): "If I should die before I wake."

Mostly, my parents showed us their faith by example. My mom was a person in whom people confided their troubles, and she frequently would send me on missions of mercy to help people she empathized with. For example, there was a mother who was very distraught because her daughter (who had a developmental disability) had no friends. She was around my age. So, it became my job to play with her even though it felt like a sacrifice since she was not very responsive, and I had to come up with all the ideas for playing.

There was another woman whose teenage daughter had caused a scandal at the same time that the family was under a great deal of stress because of the death of her husband. I was sent to ride my bike over and play with the younger daughter, who was my age. That was a joy since she was a clever, fun-loving child who just needed a change of pace. She had lots of creative ideas for making playing together a treat. Sometimes I was Lois Lane, and she was Superman from the planet Krypton. A pine cone was the dangerous green substance, Kryptonite. Sometimes the boulders in the yard were Mars and Saturn, and if we missed one when we were jumping from rock to rock, we were lost in space at least until lunchtime.

My mother also sent me to show love to a woman whose older son was going to prison. The woman was so touched by the love of our family and confided in me that everyone else was shunning her and life was painful. We all loved her so much, and I know she felt it. We are still in touch with her younger son.

One of the neighbor kids, John, who my brother met in kindergarten, told me that a lot of the parenting he had in his life was from my parents. He would eat at our house or sleep over as much as he wanted.

Yesterday, I had fun comparing notes of our 1950s memories of my parents with John. Here is what he said, starting with a memory from when he was 6:

"I remember . . . the love and kindness your mother showed me one day when I came over to your house on Chevy Chase Drive. (Circa 1957). She noticed that I had ripped my pants at the knee, and a little blood was coming out. She was very concerned that it would get infected and immediately got out a washcloth and the first aid kit to clean my knee and put a band-aid on it . . . That is, of course, something I would expect *my* mother to do . . . be concerned about me and my health . . . but not necessarily a neighborhood mom . . . Pat didn't treat me like a neighborhood kid. That day and many other days, she was my MOM.

"Your brother and I had a running Monopoly game going on each week for quite some time. Pat would sometimes come and clean the room, being very careful not to disturb our game.

"I and the neighborhood kids who lived on Chevy Chase were very fond of Bob and Pat because they were so warm and gracious. Bob and Pat were a step above other parents in their kindness, generosity, and thoughtfulness. Looking back, I'm sure it wasn't easy to raise four children and then have another neighborhood kid come and be the fifth child. But they took it all in stride, and I'm so glad that I was part of that family."

As an honorary member of the family, John sometimes took a turn picking a special dessert that my mom would bake. There is a famous legend in our family involving the chosen dessert of hot blueberry pie, John's white pants, and my youngest sister, Carol. Fortunately, my mom also helped John with his laundry. She made sure he had ironed clothes and combed hair for special occasions like First Communion or Confirmation.

Along with the rest of us, John got haircuts from my dad. When John grew up, he followed in my dad's footsteps by becoming a certified public accountant, getting a Master's Degree in Business, and being handy at home building. As grade school boys, John and my brother learned carpentry skills when they helped my frugal dad and two U of I architecture students—who my dad recruited to build our new house.

"As an honorary member of the family, John sometimes took a turn picking a special dessert that my mom would bake."

My dad taught by example. Once, he ran a stop sign. He stopped the white station wagon with me and all my siblings in it and apologized very sincerely. He told us that this was wrong and that he would try to never do it again.

He also modeled loving people of all colors and religions. When he was talking to a man with brown skin, I asked him, "How does that man know when he needs a bath?" I was very puzzled since I only knew I needed a bath when my skin turned brown from playing in the sandbox.

My dad said, "Ask him."

The man with brown skin said, "I need a bath when I start to stink."

They laughed so hard together because I didn't know people stank. My dad taught me to greet and talk to everyone we met as we walked along. A stranger was a friend we hadn't met.

My mom and dad taught us to love education. We watched them as they worked on their master's degrees. I sat on the cement floor of a tiny, windowless room off our carport, playing jacks so I could be near my dad while he typed his thesis on an old typewriter. And I sat on the floor in the stacks of the university library, coloring and smelling the leather volumes while my dad found articles for the papers he was writing.

Riding my dad's shoulders in the '50s.

While we went to school, Mom went to school too, taking Master of Education classes at U of I. After school, my mom frequently took us to the downtown public library. We brought home bags of books. I read *The Boxcar Children* series behind the brown couch in the living room, the only quiet place to be found in the noisy, happy home of my childhood.

Home Again Moment

My mom and dad taught by example. Albert Bandura, a Stanford psychologist, showed us through his research the importance of modeling for social learning. We all have models of prosocial and antisocial behavior in our lives. What a treasure it is to remember the example of people who knew how to make a home.

Home Again Questions

What stood out, struck you, or moved you in this chapter?

Who are examples to you of making a welcoming, open-hearted home? What are ways that you follow their example?

For Further Reflection

Thinking back on your own life, when have you tried to be a model to others of a welcoming, comforting presence? Journal about it and share it with someone else.

12

Grandma Angelina Esposito Recine's Homemaking

Angelina and Sam Recine with Lou.

"Mahn gi de gon!" (spelled phonetically) was the first thing I ever heard Angelina Esposito Recine say. Her translation of this for us: "This shouldn't even happen to a dog!" Then she said to my then fiancé, "You looka like a garbage man!" because she disapproved of his beard.

My husband just smiled and hugged her and kissed both her cheeks. She smiled and shook her head.

My husband Lou's grandmother Angelina raised him in his early years because his mother died a few months after he was born. Angelina Esposito Recine had come over from a farm near Naples, Italy, in 1919 at the age of 19, and she soon married Saverio (Sam) Recine (pronounced Rechenay in Italian). They were rich in industriousness and grounded in a hopeful immigrant culture, even though they lived through the Great Depression.

She told me that she ran a strict home and kept her kids on the path of hard work and clean Catholic living even when some of her friends' kids were joining the Chicago Italian mob. She told her children, "You spitta up in the air, it comma down in your face!" She was friends with mothers who had sons who had joined the mob. These wayward kids in the Mafia showed respect to Lou's grandma, visited her when she was sick, and came to her funeral dressed to show their respects in their tailored pin-striped suits and polished shoes.

When we drove from Madison and visited Lou's grandparents' brick home in an Italian Chicago neighborhood for the first time in 1976, it was a part of America I had never experienced. The home was stunningly clean, with not a weed in the tomato basil garden in the backyard. The living room furniture had clear plastic covers and looked like something out of an ornate Italian villa. The homemade noodles hung over the bed, drying. And toddler-sized Catholic saint statues were everywhere. The basement had an actively used wine vat, and sausage-making was in progress. Angelina and her husband, Saverio (Sam), who was an excellent cook, worked in the steamy kitchen together, stirring the noodles and the savory red sauce.

It was clear she was making an exception for me and welcoming me as her treasured grandchild's fiancé because "At least you looka

Italian." This was important because the Italian neighbors could see me come in and out of the home. Fortunately, I had taken Italian in college, so I could communicate with her when she spoke an Italian-laden form of broken English.

Grandma Angelina and Grandpa Sam's way of showing love was cooking. When I ate their multiple-course meal on beautiful dishes with a table full of future in-laws waving their hands and speaking in Italian, the food was heavenly. There was no sternness about manners but a certain sternness about appetites. "Mange! Mange, you're too skinny!" And when people would shout, "No, ma!" to more courses, she would yell back from the kitchen, "I no hear!" They brought "nothin' says lovin' like somethin' from the oven" to an art form with the red gravy made from the basil, parsley, and tomatoes from their garden and their Chicken Cacciatore and homemade wine.

"Anna, you standa me! You standa me?!" Even though I had taken a semester of Italian, it was hard to understand her Italian-English mixture of words without a lot of repeating on her part. She taught me this recipe (which she carried with her in her memory as she came through Ellis Island at age 19) while she was shaking her fist:

Recipe: Grandma's Meatball Recipe

Form into "medium stand-up soft" balls and fry: a mixture of 1 pound of ground meat, 2 eggs, chopped basil, garlic, breadcrumbs, parsley, and salt and pepper to taste. Then simmer in tomato sauce for 1 hour. (Her sauce was just tomato paste and water or chopped tomatoes, olive oil, garlic, parsley, and salt, simmered for 2 hours.) About halfway through the simmering time, add meatballs.

Recipe: Auntie's Red Gravy Recipe

Auntie MaryAnn (Grandma's daughter) recommends this recipe for making sauce by sautéing chopped celery, onion, and garlic in olive oil. Add two 28 ounce cans of chopped tomatoes, salt, pepper, granulated garlic, chopped parsley, and basil, and simmer for 3 hours. Just be sure to stir it so it doesn't burn. And you can do it without meat or even use pot roast for the meat in the sauce. You can add Parmesan cheese.

After we were married, regular shipments of shoe boxes (wrapped in brown paper and tied up with string) were mailed from Chicago to our Madison and, later, our Eau Claire address. They were full of homemade sausage and anisette biscotti and came with a loving note to my husband from his grandmother. Here is her Biscotti Recipe.

Recipe: Recine Biscotti

Mix 5 eggs, 1 cup of sugar, 1 softened stick of butter, and 2 teaspoons of whiskey, vanilla, or anisette extract. Then, in a separate bowl, mix 4 ½ cups of white flour, ½ teaspoon of salt (optional), and 5 teaspoons of baking powder. Mix wet and dry ingredients and form into 3 long rows (or loaves). Bake at 350 degrees Fahrenheit for 10 minutes or until golden brown (on a greased cookie sheet). Watch them carefully so they don't burn. While warm, cut on a slant. Then put the biscotti back in the oven that is turned up to 450 and quickly toast them on both sides, watching carefully so they don't burn.

She also showed her love through tears and imploring. Lou called her "long distance" every week, which at the time was expensive. She would sob on the phone because she missed him. We would drive there from Wisconsin with our small children twice a year, and she and Lou's dad and stepmom would come and stay with us once a year. She told Lou, "I cannot die until you become Catholic." She frequently begged my husband, who had been baptized Catholic as a baby, to return to the Church. In 1992, after he was confirmed in Immaculate Conception Catholic Church on the Eastside Hill, she said, "Ehh, do whatever you want to do!" acting as if she had never pressured him.

Her way of showing love was to struggle through the language barrier, tell me stories, teach me recipes, and show me how to clean clothes and garden. We got close. I knew she had fully accepted me into her home when she shared stories of unusual things that had happened to her. She complained to me that people made fun of her when she told them these stories. She would confide them to me because she said, "No one believe-a-me, but I know you believe-a-me Anna."

Enter St. Anthony of Padua.

Her oldest son, Lou's dad (also named Louis), had been deployed in World War II. She told me that she had a special devotion to St. Anthony of Padua, the early Franciscan saint who is often depicted as holding the baby Jesus. She contributed money to a St. Anthony orphanage in Italy. She implored this saint to pray for her son, Louis, "that my son comma backa no scratch" from the war. He was repairing airplanes in England during the German bombing campaign. She said that St. Anthony appeared to her. Yes, she said he appeared to her in person (not a dream) and told her that if she would stop bothering her parish priest to put her nameplate on her pew at church, "her son will comma backa no scratch."

She told me that she had worked hard to pay for that nameplate. She would take the bus to church and give the priest a piece of her mind every Sunday after Mass because he hadn't put her nameplate on the pew. This was not hard to believe. Anyone who knew Angelina Recine knows the real miracle here is that she stopped bothering the priest. Yeah, he probably had been talking to St. Anthony, too! Her son did "comma backa no scratch."

"Her way of showing love was to struggle through the language barrier, tell me stories, teach me recipes, and show me how to clean clothes and garden."

"Do you believa me, Anna?" Yes, this is an unusual story. Nevertheless, I believed her because I loved her and knew her ways. Even though Grandma told me, "Italian people are the besta people," she loved me and was patient with me as she tried to help me understand her and her homemaking traditions.

Home Again Moment

Some people show their love through giving gifts, some through acts of service, such as cooking or yard work, and others through words, or unspoken words with tears and smiles. My husband showed his love for his grandmother by hugging and kissing her and making an effort, as long as she was alive, to spend time with her on the phone and to drive to Chicago to see her.

Home Again Questions

What stood out, struck you, or moved you in this chapter?

What are your favorite ways to receive and give love?

For Further Reflection

Your favorite ways to receive and give love may not be the favorite ways of your loved ones. It's helpful to ask your loved ones, "How do you like others to show love to you?"

13

How a Home of Hospitality Changed My Worldview

In 1964, when I was twelve, my family moved from the Midwest to New England. I cried as we drove in our white station wagon away from Champaign, Illinois, a place my mother called "God's country." All our friends and most of our relatives were in Illinois. I would start to cry when "Ferry Cross the Mersey" (a song about homesickness and longing) would come on the radio. We were going away from the Midwest, the place that had formed my worldview up until then. We were leaving the place we wanted to stay in, the flat farmland of Illinois, where you could stand and see 360 degrees of the horizon. The hills, woods, and Atlantic seaside rocks and sand surrounding Boston and its culture were a big change. Going from the comfort of our small Midwestern St. Matthew's Catholic School to what my parents called a "public school" was confusing, especially for my littlest sister, Carol, who asked my mom if we would be going to "public church," too.

In the middle of my seventh-grade year, I went from a classroom of 20 kids I had known most of my life to a very large public school in Winchester, Massachusetts. "Mom, three kids said hi to me." I began to wonder if other kids were going home to their moms and counting the number of kids who said "hi" to them, so I learned as many names as I could of the class of hundreds of seventh graders. I would say hi to everyone by name as I moved in the crowded halls between classes. My tongue was like a rapid-fire jackhammer: "Hi Steve! Hi Judy! Hi Dave! Hi Kelly! . . . " Some kids were going "steady" and giving each other promise rings. Some were smoking. Some were even stealing and forming cliques. I wanted to be friends with these kids but didn't feel quite at home with most of them.

Having been raised Catholic, my worldview had not encompassed many people outside of my Catholic school and neighborhood, and it was hard to feel at home with kids who did not share my values. Yet there were some kids, like Judy, Barbie, Julie, and Betty, who I discovered were kind and good and loved their families, and I felt comfortable with them. But not enough to get the nerve to call them over the summer. So, I had a lonely summer after seventh grade.

I was so happy when the phone rang toward the end of summer, and Judy Snow invited me to hang out. We met and walked a few miles through the old neighborhoods of colonial houses to downtown Winchester and bought marshmallow fudge and penuche fudge at Brigham's Ice Cream and Candy Shop. On the way to her house, we ate the fudge at little stops by rocks or hitching posts in front of the 18th-century New England homes. We made place mats and table settings out of leaves for our picnic.

When we got to her house, we drank cider and climbed their old Copper Beech tree, from which we could see a view of the distant Boston skyline. Her 9-year-old sister was making dolls out of chestnuts and toothpicks. Her family's more than a century-old New England farmhouse, with its large open fireplace and old brick floor in the kitchen, became a place of hospitality to me. The house was filled with classical music and pipe smoke. Her parents, who sometimes "made out" in the kitchen, welcomed me into the light and love of their home. (OK, about the "making out": it was just affectionate kissing and hugging.) Judy told me that one time, when her middle-aged parents were shopping for bed sheets, a store clerk mistook them for newlyweds. Their home felt like we were in the home of newlyweds. Anyway, I was always welcome at the dinner table and overnight. During summers, I also visited them in New Hampshire at their Little Lake Sunapee cottage, which smelled like bacon, eggs, moss, and ferns.

They not only welcomed me into their home but welcomed my parents, too. Judy understood when she met me that my parents were probably lonely, too, since we were newcomers to Winchester. She said, "We have to get our parents together." We planned a dinner, and they met and became best friends. Our moms were born in the same month of the same year and sometimes celebrated their birthdays together. Our fathers had Harvard in common since Judy's dad spent a lot of time in the Harvard Yard in his undergrad days tossing a "can cover" back and forth (like throwing a Frisbee), and my dad parked his car in the Harvard Yard as he worked for many years as Harvard's Director of Research contracts. They both loved classical music and would take us to organ concerts at the Harvard Church, during which we tried their patience by giggling through the performances.

I truly experienced hospitality at their home, and they never complained (at least not very much) when I ate too many cookies, accidentally used her father's toothbrush, or said something that hurt someone's feelings. Once, I wept when I arrived at their summer place at the sight of the dimples on Judy's mother's face.

Since I had been raised partly by nuns, who passed on to me a skeptical attitude about those other Christians in our neighborhood who went to public schools, otherwise known as Lutherans, becoming part of this home of Judy's (who had become an atheist in grade school) was an important part of my development. My worldview changed by experiencing the goodness of people who did not share my faith.

"When we got to her house, we drank cider and climbed their old Copper Beech tree, from which we could see a view of the distant Boston skyline."

I loved sitting with them around their old wooden table by the kitchen fire, eating Johnny Marzetti pasta casserole or Sunapee Hermit spice cookies. Sometimes, our families ate Thanksgiving together in their formal dining room. Here is a favorite dish of her grandmother, Mimi. I was convinced the recipe came over on the Mayflower since both her parents trace their ancestry to pilgrims who landed in Massachusetts in 1620. I could picture this most New Englandy of all desserts topping off the first Thanksgiving with the Native Americans, after the turkey. My recipe card is in Mimi's handwriting.

Judy's father had been raised high church Episcopalian, but his connection to his faith faltered when he came back from World War II. He had been an officer in the landing of Allied troops from Africa into Europe and a brave leader in the bloody fight through Italy and the surrender of Germany. After risking his life, seeing so many of his brave men die, and receiving a Silver Star, he came back home and was proud of his troops, notwithstanding his Episcopalian clergy brother-in-law and sister who opposed WWII. He was shell-shocked and had a short,

Recipe: Mimi's Thanksgiving Pudding

Mix 1 cup of finely chopped suet, 1 cup of molasses, and 1 cup of milk. In a separate bowl, combine 3 cups of sifted flour, 1 teaspoon baking soda, 1¼ teaspoons salt, ½ teaspoon ginger, ½ teaspoon ground cloves, and 1 teaspoon cinnamon, and add to wet ingredients. Mix in 1½ cups of lightly floured raisins. Butter a pudding mold, pour in the mixture, and steam for 3 hours. (I would google what can be used as a "pudding mold" and how to gently steam in a saucepan if you have never done it.) Serve with Hard Sauce: Made with ½ cup of soft butter creamed with 2 Tablespoons of "good" brandy and 2 cups of confectioners (powdered) sugar.

failed marriage before he discovered the love of his life, Nancy Nutter, a dear longtime friend of his family.

Judy's strikingly beautiful brunette mother, Nancy, had been raised Unitarian. Even though I enjoyed the sugar cookies and hot tea at the Unitarian festival at Christmas, I was puzzled that Judy's Sunday School teachers did not seem to have much to say about God. So Judy, at a young age, was given the choice by the grown-ups around her to believe whatever she came up with. It is not surprising that God was not in the picture. I still passionately believed in God during my junior high and high school years, but the Snows' hospitality helped me to also passionately believe in them.

My mom used to talk about some people being "provincial," meaning that attachment to their own place or province gave them a narrow worldview. My narrow worldview of believing that the Midwest Catholic families I loved were the best people expanded to believing in the goodness of People (with a capital "P") when I met this wonderful family in New England. Their home became my home, too.

Judy's dad and me in the 1960s.

Judy and me with my dad in Winchester at a fair.

Home Again Moment

When kids go to a new school they often do not feel a sense of belonging that first week, but before long, they find a sense of belonging with others that may last their whole lives. *That can be true of being a newcomer anywhere.* The process of going from newcomer to a sense of belonging is partly dependent on the hospitality of others.

Home Again Questions

What stood out, struck you, or moved you in this chapter?

How can each of us be like this New England family and help newcomers gain a sense of belonging?

For Further Reflection

Some people can run a three-ring circus, and some can only occasionally get one ring going. Offering to share a meal with someone at a restaurant, even if you go Dutch and bring a coupon for them, or stopping to chat with someone are simple ways to be a welcoming presence, even if you are not up to having guests. A friendly text or call can mean a lot.

14

How a Home of Hospitality Changed My Worldview Again

In 1972, when I was 19, hospitality in the home of Dr. Amun and Deidre Gobran changed my worldview again. This is a story of a sudden eye-opening experience that felt like getting off a plane in a friendly southern climate after the bitter winter of the north. Life at that time felt like a tiring task: trying to do all the things for myself that my parents had done for me, working in a hospital, and trying to figure out life. I felt worn out and had a vague longing, a coming-of-age search for meaning.

By that time in my life, I was at the developmental stage in which I did not accept or reject the values of my upbringing. I did not believe or disbelieve in God. They say God has no grandchildren, only children. So, figuring out what I believed was not a process of mimicking what my parents believed but of sorting out myself and seeking. Around that time, I made a poster that accidentally offended a close friend. He said it was too religious. It had a painting of a door, and it said, "Seek, and you shall find: knock, and it shall be opened to you." I didn't know what I believed, but that poster expressed a longing.

I lived in Cambridge, Massachusetts, and started going to the Harvard church, which was biking distance away. My father, a naturally eloquent speaker, had been a volunteer lay preacher there on his lunch breaks when he worked at Harvard as a research contract negotiator in the '60s. This familiar space of the beautiful old red brick church with the tall white steeple towering over the trees in the Harvard Yard felt like home. When I biked there, I listened to the hymns but not the sermons. The words and music of the ancient hymns and the familiarity of the magnificent organ spoke to me. My memories of going to organ recitals with my father, Judy, and her father in this space (I sat in the same polished and worn wooden pews we had sat in during the concerts) stirred a desire for something I could not name. I now realize I was homesick.

In the summer of 1972, I walked along the Charles River with a 20-year-old friend of mine, Jonathan. He was a Boston musician who had his first record out. He told me his band was named The Modern Lovers because they loved the modern world that was getting a bad rap. Even though he was well known enough in Boston to have a write-up in *The Harvard Crimson* student paper about his songwriting, the band still played sometimes in nursing homes and high school gyms. I met him when he played in a nearly empty high school gym in Cambridge. He caused me to want to examine my worldview. He also believed that honest seeking, asking, and knocking were important.

As we walked along the Charles riverside at twilight with the lights of the Boston skyline reflecting in the water, Jonathan asked me powerful questions that piqued my curiosity, such as, "Have you experienced ontological wonder? Will we live in such a way that we have dignity when we are in our seventies? Are we, or any of our heroes, living in the kingdom of God?" He told me he became a musician partly because, on a trip to Israel as a Jewish teen, he had a realization that helped him believe he could do something meaningful through rock and roll music. He inspired me to think about ways I might want to change the direction of my life.

I was in a frame of mind of letting go of the old me (even though the old me wasn't very old) and opening myself to something new. I had missed the fall deadline to return to classes at the University of Wisconsin–Madison after taking a year off to work in a Boston hospital and trying to figure out what I wanted to be when I grew up. Still unsure of my direction, I stood on the side of a road in the early evening of September 9, 1972, wearing a trench coat and putting my thumb out for a ride.

I was hitchhiking from Winchester to Cambridge by the Mystic Lakes. I was beginning to consider reconnecting with God, but I had two problems. On one hand, I was blaming God for not making a better world. Unlike Jonathan, I didn't love the modern world where I was afraid to take the subway because I had heard that 30-ish women a night were attacked in Boston, so I had ridden my bike in the snow to and from work on the night shift. I was disappointed with God. On the other hand, from the words of the hymns at the Harvard church and talks with friends who were following a guru from India, I was inspired to seek personal holiness. This is harder than it sounds. I was disappointed with myself, too.

Even my 19-year-old self knew that the safety of hitchhiking was dubious, but I didn't have a car, and Boston's MTA train took too much planning, had too many transfers, and the risk of danger in the underground stations. A bit nervously, I prayed that the first car would pick me up and the people would be kind and loving. Dr. Amun Gobran slammed on the brakes of his car and put it in reverse. I got in the back seat. He and his wife, Deidre, asked me compassionate questions that brought tears to my eyes that I didn't want them to notice. Even though we had never met, by the time they took me to my rooming house near Harvard, they suggested that I come home with them instead of being dropped off in my dangerous neighborhood. I felt very comfortable with them. I actually felt safer with them than with the mysterious people in the rooming house I had just moved into. *They* were scary. Amun was a Harvard Med School professor, and Deidre had just started a hospice unit at a Boston hospital. I clicked with them. They felt like "my people."

I was curious about these kind, highly educated people—Amun with his thick Egyptian accent and Deidre with charming Britishisms. They seemed very curious about me, too, for a reason that I found out a year later. I'll explain shortly. I trusted them enough to say "yes." They had told me enough in the conversation to make me think they were pretty safe: after all, he was a professor, and she was a nurse!

"It was late, but Deidre served tea and biscuits (cookies). And Amun, a doctor, listened to me in their tiny but cozy apartment . . . "

It was late, but Deidre served tea and biscuits (cookies). And Amun, a doctor, listened to me in their tiny but cozy apartment in Arlington, one town west of Cambridge in the Metropolitan Area. He told me he was a Coptic Christian, an ancient form of Christianity in Egypt, and Deidre said she had been an English Salvation Army worker. Since they were clearly religious, I asked them very sincerely, "If God is so good, why is there so much evil in the world?"

Amun said, in his deep voice with his Egyptian accent, "God is so good that he doesn't take away a gift when he gives it. The gift of free will makes love possible." This had the surprising effect of causing me to become more tentative about my grudge against God.

To further explain God's response to evil in the world, he told me a story that I still remember 50-some years later: "Once there was a general who had a son who had stolen. The general was a just man and announced that his son should receive the usual military punishment and be brought to the courtyard at dawn to be beaten. The next morning, when his son was brought to the courtyard and had his hands tied behind his back, the heart of the general was moved with compassion. He said, 'Untie him and tie me in his place, and I will be beaten.'"

I really listened. I thought hard about it. The story was inspiring to me. I understood (for what felt like the first time) the depth of what Jesus did for me on the cross. This realization gave me the feeling of resting in the sun with the wind in my hair after a long convalescence. The sound of their voices had qualities of health, beauty, and wisdom as we talked about this until late at night.

The hospitality of their home changed my worldview, even though I didn't mention it to them before I left the next morning. It was too enormous, personal, and difficult to express what had happened. It would take time to put it into words.

I wanted to make a change. I felt I was like Dorothy in *The Wizard of Oz*—I had a strong desire to click my heels together and go home to Madison. After phoning my parents and talking it over with Jonathan and my brother, I flew home to Wisconsin with the aim of going to nursing school. My grades were good from my first year there, but because I was late, I needed some special permissions to join the classes. I was relieved that the dean of the Nursing School gave the thumbs up. I wanted to be a nurse, but it was still a shock to me to suddenly be in nursing school catching up on all my classes (including Chemistry and Microbiology) within the week of my visit to the Gobrans' home.

I tried to tell my dad about this hitchhiking experience that changed my life and what happened in Dr. Amun and Deidre's home. He told me he did not want to hear about it. Probably to preserve his sanity, he maintained a respectful distance from the exciting stories of his teenage children, especially the risk-taking experiences like hitchhiking and going to a stranger's house for a sleepover. (I should have known better. Since distressing my father usually resulted in a few hours of him processing the news by sitting at our baby grand piano and filling the house with improvised music in downcast minor keys.)

The next spring, he said to me, "You have made a 180-degree turnaround in your life. I am going to Boston for a seminar, and I want to meet Dr. Amun and Deidre." Over the year of living at home and going to college, I had changed my know-it-all teen attitude to one of very sincere, respectful deference to my father. We were developing a closer relationship through walking our black and white collie-like dog, Spooky, in our Madison west side neighborhood off Mineral Point Road.

On our after-supper strolls, we had long talks about ethics and especially his admiration of Dr. Martin Luther King Jr. My dad used one-to-one chats on walks to pass on his values to all four of his favorite children. It was clear to all of us that our father was a very good, moral man. And we listened to him. At that point in his life, he was a churchgoing agnostic, appreciating the ethical teaching of the priest at the university's Newman Foundation on State Street, but not sure of the reality of God.

In the cold spring of 1973, Mom, Dad, and I drove from Wisconsin to Massachusetts, and soon I was sitting in the downtown Boston Hilton Hotel's dining room with its old high ceiling, chandeliers, and white tablecloths with my parents, Dr. Gobran, and Deidre. The dining room looked like a scene from the Harry Potter movie set in the

Great Hall in Hogwarts Castle. I was in the "seen but not heard" mode, not knowing what would happen. Even though they had just met, soon they were talking like old friends. My father and Amun were shooting the breeze about medical ethics when my father asked, "Why did you pick her up hitchhiking?"

Amun's olive-skinned face turned pale, and he assured my father that he was a normal man. And then he said, "My wife and I had never picked up a hitchhiker before. We usually sing hymns in the car and try to grab a little time together. I don't know if it was God or an angel, but I heard a voice saying, 'Stop the car and pick up this girl!'" Tears rolled down my parents' faces, and it was clear that my father believed him. I acknowledge and value that not everyone, upon hearing this narrative, would believe it. However, my parents' response was quite different.

The experience piqued my dad's intellectual curiosity. When he got back to Madison, he began reading *Mere Christianity* by C. S. Lewis (of Narnia fame) and said the book made sense to him.

My atheist friend, Judy Snow (now Judy Nations), whose family I described in the previous chapter, also believed me when I told her the story. She began asking me questions about how my worldview changed, which she felt was against her better judgment since she really did not want to know more; but then again, she did. Her worldview changed, too, which led her to get a Master's Degree in Theology and marry a Presbyterian pastor. (There is so much more to tell about what happened when her worldview changed, but that doesn't come into this story. She wrote about it in her book *Quite The Journey*.)

Home Again Moment

As we think back on our lives, we realize there might be so many people we would like to thank! The next year, after meeting the Gobrans, I made a trip to New England to thank them in person since they had no idea how much they had helped me. There is a lot of research on gratitude and how expressing it brings measurable happiness to our lives. That was a happy reunion that I still treasure.

Home Again Questions

What stood out, struck you, or moved you in this chapter?

Can you think of someone who made a deep impression on you and helped you to find your way when you were struggling? Or anyone who helped you in your life, even in a small way? Have you thanked them? If so, what did you do, and how did that feel to you? If not, how can you best express your gratitude to them?

For Further Reflection

Research from the University of Pennsylvania on writing a gratitude letter and reading it face-to-face to the person you want to thank shows how a simple activity can bring long-lasting happiness. Instructions can be found at the website for The Greater Good in Action:
https://ggia.berkeley.edu/practice/practice_as_pdf/
gratitude_letter

15

Bob and Pat Gentry Day

My mom and dad.

Yes, my parents had a day named after them. Really! I will explain.

When we were young, my dad would have us go to a big old leather-bound dictionary and look up words like "stereospecificity" and "philoprogenitive" (the latter of which we learned meant love of offspring). As my parents, Bob and Pat Gentry, aged, they treated their whole community as their offspring whom they loved. They did it with brownies, a lawn mower, and the use of their gifts of hospitality and administrative skills. They never picked up the East Coast accents of their neighbors, but they became a beautiful addition to Danbury, Connecticut, with their Midwestern hospitality and work ethic.

When my mom and dad moved to Danbury in their 50s, my dad had just lost his job at a religious university after refusing, as Vice President for Finance, to allow what he called "circumventing the IRS." So, he took a job in Danbury to do financial work for Boehringer Ingelheim Pharmaceutical Company.

He told me that when he got to Danbury, discouraged by ill-treatment for doing the ethical thing at his last job, he prayed that for the rest of his life he would do whatever Jesus Christ wanted him to do. Not knowing anyone in Danbury, he started his mission to serve Christ there by calling an agency and asking them to give him the name of a woman in a nursing home who had no family so he could become her visitor. Her name was Alice.

He continued to visit her after she was discharged to her home. When he took Alice to visit her husband's grave in the Kenosha Cemetery near his house, he was annoyed that elderly people had to walk through tall grass in an unmown cemetery. So, he started mowing the cemetery. When he noticed the same problem all over the city, he started a Danbury Cemetery Association, a group of volunteers to care for and organize the cemeteries. When he died, they gave him a free grave in the Kenosha Cemetery.

He put Alice's mailbox back up on its post and did other house maintenance for her. Then, he recruited the Boy Scouts and men's clubs to do repairs on the houses of the elderly all over the community. He also organized groups of volunteers to drive care packages to military ships in the nearby port to cheer up soldiers.

He was accustomed to living in clean Wisconsin, and he told me he wanted to teach the people in the community to take pride in keeping Danbury clean. He put on gloves and picked up litter on the streets of his neighborhood with a stick he made with a nail on the end. Then he went door to door to clinics and other organizations, asking them to commit to regularly picking up the litter on sections of roads and highways near their offices. He and my mom made a video for the schools to teach children not to litter. Then he went on to the New England Governors' Conference, where he spoke to them about starting Adopt-A-Highway projects in their states. By the way, my dad's priest (who loved my dad and in later years often visited him in the hospital) told me that on his first day in the rectory, the first person coming up his walk was my beloved dad, and the first greeting out of my dad's mouth was an exhortation to the young priest to pick up the litter in his yard.

The mayor's mother sat next to my parents at church, and he would pass messages to the mayor through his mom on his ideas for volunteer projects. He bugged the mayor so much about needs in the community that the mayor gave my dad an office at city hall, letterhead, and placed him in charge of volunteer services. It was Dad's way of serving Jesus Christ.

My parents were a good match; they both lived generously. In their own quiet way, they tried to follow their faith, whether it was in the church, at City Hall, at men's club, women's club, in the neighborhood, or in their home.

They reached beyond their doors to help make Danbury, Connecticut, a homey place. My mom had so much company in their house over the years that we said she had a PhD in hospitality. She organized the tiny Danbury Women's Club into a dynamo when she was president and mentored the future presidents, starting lots of special activities in the club for women with a variety of interests, whether it be books, hiking, or crafts. The women of the Danbury Women's Club, under my mother's leadership, proudly made their presence known at city parades and in charitable fundraising for needs in the city.

My mother was actually the "grandmother" who was the first person to hold the baby of a single mom in the neighborhood whose own family did not make it in time to be at the birth. And there was a beautiful 40-something back-door neighbor who told me that when her son would come home on breaks from college, he would go over to my parents' house to do anything he saw that needed to be done in the yard because they had been like grandparents to him.

On my parents' 50th wedding anniversary, February 11, the mayor made a proclamation that henceforth, February 11 would be *Bob and Pat Gentry Day* in Danbury.

"My parents were a good match; they both lived generously."

And not to be outdone, the priest had a proclamation from the Pope to present to them, honoring their marriage. The priest was grateful for my dad's gifts of financial administration, which was my dad's way of serving Christ in his church. As the senior member of the finance committee of St. Peter Catholic Church in downtown Danbury, my dad managed to get the church in the black after years of financial deficit. The priest hated the arguing in the finance committee meetings. When my dad joined, it stopped. Everyone listened and obeyed his sage advice, and it enabled a large old downtown church (that served immigrants with Masses in three to four different languages) to stay open. My dad had managed finances for the University of Wisconsin, Harvard, and other universities and knew how to add common sense, thrift, priorities, and good math together to keep his home solvent and to bring a sense of stability to a community.

To our surprise, when he died, the Connecticut Senate sent regards and a proclamation signed by many senators thanking him for all he did for Connecticut. We all came home to plan the funeral. My mom was in her 80s. Part of Mom's plan was to invite everyone who came to the funeral Mass back to the house for a meal. I asked, "How many people will we be feeding?" She said, "About 70." I asked if she planned to cater it. No, the plan was that we would all make the meal. This was natural for my mother, who was used to cooking for large groups of people who came to her house for lunches and brunch. But this is not what happened.

What happened instead is that the Danbury Women's Club got wind of the plan and wouldn't have it. They were grateful for all my mom had done for the community when she was president of the club. They stationed a posse of women at our house who prepared a feast while others were at the funeral, so we came home to a dining table spread with food that they forbade my mother and her four children to help with. The meal was amazing. It was the first time I had Greek watermelon salad. It is not an immediately obvious combination, but the watermelon, cucumber, olive, and feta salad was truly special comfort food on that difficult occasion.

Recipe: Greek Watermelon Salad

Toss the following with red wine vinegar, olive oil, salt, and pepper in a BIG bowl:

3-4 cups chopped watermelon

2 chopped large tomatoes

1 chopped cucumber.

Some chopped parsley and mint.

1 chopped red onion

¾ cup pitted kalamata olives

¾ cup crumbled feta.

My cousins came to the funeral, and one of them, an agriculture professor, told me that over the years, he had slept in every bedroom in the house. He said this when we tried to trade bedrooms with him at my mother's urging because she wanted the guests to have the best bedrooms. When he and his sister had arrived late the previous evening, they had taken the only room left. It was a small attic room decorated for young children, with lots of large toy trucks, cars, airplanes, stuffed bears, and dolls. It had two low single beds covered in bright quilts. It was a room with a history.

In October of 2012 (before Dad died) during Hurricane Sandy, that little room was a busy place of hospitality. There was, of course, no school. The doorbell would ring frequently. The little boys in the neighborhood would come over to play in that room. During the stress of having no heat, water, landlines, or electricity, the little children's happy voices and trick-or-treating brought joy to my parents.

It was time for all the neighbors who had received my parents' brownies, hospitality, and help over the years to give something back. Fortunately, I answered the door since my selfless mother would have been too shy to accept help when she was so used to being the giver. When they asked *me* if my parents needed anything, I had my list ready. But more about that later. They not only helped us with supplies but each one had heartfelt praise for my parents.

Neither of my parents ever sought the honors that their community gave them. They just liked to work together to make their community a better home for many. That's why Danbury proclaimed their anniversary as *Bob and Pat Gentry Day*!

Home Again Moment

My dad started with one little way to serve his community by visiting Alice, someone who didn't have any visitors. My mom started by inviting one person over. It was like the beginning of making a snow fort. It starts with one snow brick. Or like dropping one pebble in a still lake, creating an oscillating circular pattern of ripples affecting the whole surface of the lake. It was what I like to call "The Little Way of Bob and Pat." Due to no fault of their own, they had to move, to start again to build a home of love in a new community. They took a simple path of using small, ordinary things to make Danbury more of a happy home for their community.

Home Again Questions

What stood out, struck you, or moved you in this chapter?

What "Little Way" of your own can you find to bring love to someone today?

For Further Reflection

My parents taught me that there is beauty in the ordinary—in watching the rain, in a hot cup of coffee, watching a fire, and especially sharing it with others. My parents did ordinary things like mowing, cooking sloppy joes, or holding hands with great love. What are "ordinary" but beautiful activities in your life that you can perform with a sense of joy and love? Who are the people with whom your life *ordinarily* intersects and with whom you can see a special beauty? How might you show loving appreciation for them?

16

Hospital Homemaking

In 1958, when I was 6 years old, I sat at my little blond desk in the back of the classroom and examined the picture I had drawn with crayons—in one of the few moments that I was paying attention in first grade. We were supposed to draw a picture of what we wanted to be when we grew up. I tried to remember what the nurses in the hospital had looked like. I wished I had given the nurse that I had drawn thicker legs than the one-line sticks. It came back from the teacher without a star.

I bonded with nurses when I was hospitalized twice as a preschooler to investigate stomach aches. Crying alone in the hospital crib, the only comfort came from nurturing young nurses who would come hold me.

In 2007, when I was studying day in and day out to take the nurse practitioner board exam, I often asked myself, "What was I thinking?" Working at a coffee shop as a barista, where the only mistake I could make would be putting in soy milk instead of oat milk, would be way less stressful than diagnosing correctly and prescribing medication. "How did I get here?"

Recently, I read a note in my friend's copy of Madison West High's 1970 yearbook. She had written next to my picture, gently chiding me for believing I could "change the world" through such a conventional means as nursing, yet cheering me on for my passion. Now, I realize as a retired nurse in my 70s that I didn't achieve any world-changing goals but only carried on a tradition passed on to me of bringing comfort and a breath of home to one patient at a time.

In 1971, when I was 18 years old after dropping out of college at the University of Wisconsin–Madison, I was in a state of confusion about what I wanted to be when I grew up. My dad was more in desperation about my confusion than I was. I thought I might like to be a nurse. Even though it was a bit of nepotism, to test out my vocational aspiration of becoming a nurse, my dad got me a job as a nursing assistant at a Harvard teaching hospital, which later became Brigham and Women's. He knew the administrator from his Harvard days. His fatherly involvement paid off because, at the end of the year, I came back to Madison with a vision to be a nurse.

I worked on a women's surgical floor where patients from both the poverty of the Boston streets and from all over the world came to be in the hands of Harvard surgeons. It was a sunny ward, one large room that had a long row of beds on each side of a middle corridor. The beds were only separated from each other by privacy curtains, which were open most of the time. Each bed had a window behind it that was frequently open to provide fresh air. The end of the ward had a door that opened to a large veranda that surrounded the ward and was full of weathered shellback painted metal chairs, so patients could go out and get fresh air and, from their third-floor perch, watch the birds and branches of the trees sway in the breeze.

During my training, experienced staff taught me both clinical skills (like how to change the sheets with someone in the bed while giving them a bath) and the basics of bringing the comforts of home to each patient. I learned to give each willing patient a back rub with lotion before sleep. We practiced the techniques of effleurage, petrissage, friction, and percussion on each other so we could learn to give the people lying in the beds a good night's sleep when we dimmed the light. Well, at least as good of a night's sleep as could be had when you could hear the music of some 20 people breathing, moaning, and coughing with interludes of the sound of staff coming in and out to take temperatures, pump blood pressure cuffs, and give medicine through the night.

"We became their temporary family, and the ward, their temporary home. These courageous women, clad in blue-striped hospital gowns and bandages, . . . were inspiring and nurturing."

Soon, I reported to the Women's Surgical Ward at 6 a.m., caffeinated and all ready for my first day, in my new size small pink uniform dress that was still too big for my slight frame and my long brown hair pinned up in braids on my head. At the bedside of my first patient, I fainted from seeing and smelling a gaping pizza-size wound. Yes, I blacked out and would have fallen if a nurse had not lowered me to a chair. But I learned to be OK with seeing and smelling the foul odor of wounds from practice because I wanted to be a part of this world. While emptying bags of urine and bedpans, changing bloody sheets, and taking temperatures, we listened to these people in the beds.

We became their temporary family, and the ward, their temporary home. These courageous women, clad in blue-striped hospital gowns and bandages, many of whom had flown here from other countries, were inspiring and nurturing. Their bodies were weak—all bearing fresh surgical incisions—but their spirits were sturdy.

I learned a recipe for Irish Soda Bread from an older woman with a lovely musical brogue, a beautiful pink complexion, and curly silver hair. Even though she was recovering from a difficult surgery, she worked hard to teach me by repeatedly tasting my attempts at her recipe that she would correct. What made her recipe so special was that it combined vanilla, caraway seeds, and currants, and was served warm with butter. It's the kind of treat that makes me want to keep having another slice whenever I walk by it. Here is her recipe with optional tweaks we have done over the years:

Recipe: Mrs. Kelly's Irish Soda Bread

Preheat the oven to 375 degrees Fahrenheit. Lightly grease a bread or cake pan or line a baking sheet with parchment paper.

Combine in a bowl: 4 cups flour, ¼ cup sugar, 1 tablespoon caraway seeds (optional), 1 teaspoon salt, 1 teaspoon baking soda, 2 teaspoons baking powder.

Mix or <u>cut</u> 4 tablespoons of cold butter into the dry ingredients. (The butter should be in pea-size crumbs. I use a pastry cutter—like making pie. A fork can work too.)

Whisk 2 eggs, 1 teaspoon vanilla or almond extract, and 1 ²/3 cups of buttermilk and Slowly mix it into the dry ingredients. (You can make a buttermilk substitute by adding a dash of white vinegar to milk.) (Optional) Add 1 cup of currants or raisins. Bake for 45 minutes in the bread or cake pan or, after forming a ball, on a cookie sheet. (Some people use a cast iron skillet or Dutch oven.) When it's golden brown, check for doneness by putting in a toothpick to see if it comes out dry. If it gets brown before it's done inside, cover it with tinfoil and continue to bake until done.

I listened to the stories of a strikingly beautiful, illiterate, young Romani woman with shiny black hair. She introduced herself as a Gypsy, and she taught me a recipe for fruit bread by telling me the size of the can or bag of flour to use. The recipe called for a number 10 can of peaches. She taught me that cans had numbers (who knew?), so reading the labels wasn't necessary. As I took care of her in that hospital bed, she poured out her troubles. She had a jealous lover who she feared would murder his rival. She was an example of turning to prayer in her troubles.

Since I was only 18 and looked much younger with my slight stature and long braid, the patients correctly decided I needed their wisdom. I received lots of advice from those lovely women in the beds on the Harvard surgical ward during the year I was there.

They had good tips: "A penny saved is a penny earned," and "Always take care of your feet. You will need them as you age."

I even received invitations, "You must come to my home to visit me when I get out of the hospital." I never took up the invitation issued passionately in Spanish and hand motions to go to the "Terra Linda" of a dark-haired beauty. But I did spend a week on the Massachusetts shore with a lonely teen whose chronic illness had stressed her ability to make friends and worn out her parents' marriage. This visit to their family home on the ocean was a planned distraction during the divorce proceedings. Nevertheless, we had a beautiful time listening to records of the Eagles (her favorite band), going to the beach, and talking about boys.

It was a different time when smoking was considered safe, and doctors passed out cigarettes at the start of the shift report conference as we discussed particularly difficult cases. We had a fraction of the procedures and medications we have now and no computer terminals that nurses and nursing assistants spend so much time at now. Yet hospital homemaking, the art of creating a nurturing caring environment for the patient, is still an important part of why young people go into nursing.

One of the ways we pass on this nursing art at the University of Wisconsin–Eau Claire is to teach students to empathize with and understand people from different cultures. We want vulnerable people to trust us as we care for them. I liked to tell my students about a depressed, middle-aged Native American patient on a psychiatric unit of an Eau Claire hospital who told me that he was waiting for me to be his nurse because he trusted that I would believe him. He told me that in his Ojibwe tribal culture, people respected and gave great significance to dreams and visions.

Through his recalling of dreams, he told me of the deep wounding his people had received from white people and his anger at the poverty of the homes on the reservation and intergenerational trauma passed on by wounded people. He needed to talk. As his story unfolded, it was not just filled with trauma but with the beautiful dignity of resilience, courage, and determination to hold onto his culture. Our patients are our teachers. The storms of his life led to our meeting and gave him insights to share on how to weather these storms.

When I was a faculty member, I read the entrance essays of young people who told the stories of why they wanted to be nurses. In these papers, they frequently talked about the storms of life that had brought them in touch with nurses. When they were away from home in this strange environment full of foreign smells, sounds, and procedures, nurses touched their lives and brought them a bit of home. They wanted to give others the nurturing and homey care they had received.

Home Again Moment

When people are sick, they need a special kind of homemaking. Think of ways that people who cared for you when you were sick brought a sense of comfort and security to you. Have you ever been able to do that for someone else? Sometimes, it's good to think in advance of ways to bring comfort to people when they are acutely or chronically ill.

How can we bring comfort to people who have been wounded by life? Edith Eger, who is sometimes called "the Anne Frank who lived," refers to the emotional wound she received in Auschwitz as "my precious wound" because it taught her that she had the power to choose to comfort the world. As a teen, she was kicked off an Olympic gymnastics team for being Jewish, torn from her home, lost her parents in the ovens of Auschwitz, and was rescued by American soldiers as she lay dying. She is an American psychologist, born in Hungary in 1927.

Edith gets standing ovations when she talks to large groups of men and women in our military suffering from PTSD. She teaches them about choice, overcoming victimhood, healing, and celebrating life. She shows us that hurting people don't have to bring their wounds into their homes as a hidden reason for hurting their families. These wounds can become a precious gift that gives us the power to bring a beautiful balm of comfort and hope.

Home Again Questions

What stood out, struck you, or moved you in this chapter?

Home Again Questions, Continued

What are your "precious wounds" that are making you into a wounded healer? How have you been able to comfort others because of the comfort you have received?

For Further Reflection

Who in your life today has challenges or needs and could benefit from your creating a nurturing, caring environment? When you plan for your week, how can you notice the need for comfort in others? What are the ways by which you can bring these comforts to them? Where do you get the inspiration to comfort people?

HOME IS . . .

17

Home Is a Place

My husband had a poignant moment alone in our living room after supper dishes last night. He said that if he knew he would die tomorrow, the two old framed prints over our couch, one of a harbor, one of a beautiful village, and a hand-me-down painting of a beach with seagulls, would become extremely precious to him. He said it helped him realize how precious they should be to him now, even though he is healthy, and how he should treasure every beautiful thing in this place *today*. I asked him to tell me why they were so precious to him. He said it is an indescribable feeling about our home, about this place on the East Hill in Eau Claire, Wisconsin.

Though I have seen many awe-inspiring places in the world through long travels, visiting them did not mean that I had actually experienced the world. I have learned to see the adventure of experiencing the world as a laborious, unassuming, hopeful excursion of less than a foot span to my own door, to my own yard.

I had a poignant experience of the joy of my feet in my own backyard when my employer, a community healthcare company, downsized. Most workers started working from home and out of their cars, doing home visits to patients. I situated my home office so I could see my backyard apple trees as I worked. I watched them change from white boughs of blossoms to a canopy of green leaves full of juicy red McIntosh apples. As I walked in the shaded grass in my yard during breaks from my work, I discovered the newness and beauty of my own place. When the sky was blue or gray, windy or calm, I would walk and be in the present moment and realize that what I was seeing would never be the same again as in this moment. Every inch of my yard was a discovery. I arrived at my own yard, at my own door. And it was beautiful and transient and joyful and humbling.

"As I walked in the shaded grass in my yard during breaks from my work, I discovered the newness and beauty of my own place."

It wasn't a walk where I judged between a wildflower and a weed or judged anything at all, like whether the grass needed cutting. It was a walk where I let go of everything in the world except the experience of this place, my place. The experience of discovering the world by staying put in my neighborhood with its weather, its bird and dog sounds, and its sky and earth sights—of staying put in my smallness.

A small bungalow on the East Hill of Eau Claire, Wisconsin, serves as my home as I travel from this life to the next. At each moment, it is full of beauty and happiness—if I do the difficult task of being in the present moment and experiencing the world of my loving Heavenly Father in this short excursion to my own door.

Home Again Moment

Is there something in your home or in your homelife that feels important or precious to you in light of the brevity of all of our lives on this planet? Or, have you ever come home after a long trip and felt a stirring of joy about something in your home or, simply, about being back home again?

Home Again Questions

What stood out, struck you, or moved you in this chapter?

What are ways you can bring yourself back to—or keep yourself in—the present moment and the beauty of your own place?

For Further Reflection

It's nice to go on a five-senses walk. As you walk along, what do you see? What do you hear? What do you smell? What do you feel? Perhaps the wind? Or a leaf? And even, you might taste something.

18

Home Is a Person

"I love to watch the fishermen! . . . What beautiful sailboats! . . . The fish are jumping!" My mom's delight in looking out the picture windows of the condo was contagious. She was in her 90s, an age when all steps feel steeper and even a long hall feels like it is going uphill, so she liked to sit and watch the sunsets over Lake Mendota in Madison, Wisconsin. She lived in a second-floor condo near the university that felt like it was part of a cruise ship because, outside the window, you could only see the lake, with its UW–Madison crew team and its Hoofer Club sailors cutting through the waves in the summer, and people ice fishing for hours in the winter.

Yet even though she found the lake quite fascinating to watch, that is *not* what made her feel at home. She told me she felt comfortable there because her things reminded her of the people she loved. When I visited, she always talked about the painting in her condo that had hung over her fireplace in the house she had shared with my father before he died. She would point out the chair in the living room that had been her mother's and the desk that had belonged to a dear, long-deceased aunt.

These objects were the treasures that made the condo feel like home. "Home is where my furniture is," she had said in reply to my sister Carol, who had once said to my mom many years earlier, "I don't know where my home is" because my parents had made so many moves to different university jobs. It wasn't because my mom loved the furniture, but something of the essence of the *people* she loved still clung to these objects. These people were her *home,* even though they were far away or gone.

I would ask her how her day went when I would call her on video chat every evening. As she became more confused toward the end of her life, she would smile and tell me how she had spent the day with my deceased dad or with her mother.

Dr. Christopher Kerr's research from interviews with over 1,400 hospice patients (who were near death) confirmed that visions of reunions with deceased loved ones are common and often comforting. Perhaps families don't talk about this much because they feel it may be part of mental illness. But apparently, it is very normal. *People near death feel that the people in their hearts are in their homes.*

Of course, home is not just a person who we loved on earth who is gone, but a home is often a special person here on earth. People feel at home in their neighborhoods, churches, or schools if they have at least one person who helps them feel comfortable.

☼☼☼

Big people and small people need that kind of person. When my daughter was a fourth grader and adjusting to her new school, she needed a person to make her feel at home.

"This is a black table; you can't sit here." My daughter's fourth-grade classmates told her this at lunchtime. This was a surprise to her. She had just started the year in a public school in South Carolina when my husband was in college there for a year. We had moved from Eau Claire, Wisconsin—where my daughter's best friend was a beautiful, clever African American neighborhood girl. The color of someone's skin had never mattered to my daughter, so her experience of being shunned in the South when she was the only girl with ivory-colored skin in her classroom was unexpected.

Her teacher had very little classroom control, kept the TV on most of the day, and smelled like alcohol. My daughter began to develop headaches from the noise of the classroom and the stress of being ostracized. She missed her classmates in the little, very orderly Catholic grade school a few blocks from our home on the East Hill in Eau Claire.

When our daughter, my husband, and I met with the principal and the teacher in the classroom, she was offered the opportunity to move to the other fourth-grade classroom, where the teacher had more control, and there was more peaceful racial integration. My daughter began to cry and said, "I can't leave." It was because of one person. One person she loved made this classroom a home for her that she could not leave in spite of the suffering. "I can't leave without Ruth."

Ruth was a girl from Nigeria whose dad went to the same college as my husband and who dressed, talked, and acted differently than the other children in the class. She was homesick, and she was mercilessly bullied. "Ruth will not survive here in this class without me." So they let Ruth go with her, and those two little girls had a jolly time. But that is a story for another book. Suffice it to say they had sleepovers, our families got together for meals, and the girls ran a city marathon together—after lots of practicing on the playground. They cheered each other on scholastically and athletically. Their achievements and their joys were so great together bullies didn't have a chance.

One night, as I was tucking our daughter in her snug little bedroom, she talked to me about her friend Ruth. She quoted the book of Ruth in the Bible. "Where you go, I will go . . . your people will be my people, and your God will be my God." Her sense of being at home in school and her adjustment to our family's year in South Carolina were greatly helped by one person. She had Ruth in her heart.

Yes, a home is a place, but it is also a person. Actor James Franco, playing the role of "Taste" (the tattooed sleeveless boyfriend of "Whippit"—played by Mila Kunis—in the screwball comedy *Date Night*), makes this point eloquently right before a big smooch scene. As the young couple makes an escape from their apartment (probably forever), a stressed-out Whippit is comforted by Taste, as he reassures her that their apartment is not their home, but she, in fact, resides in his heart, her true home. He shows her a tattoo of her face on his chest and pounds it with his fist, saying, "This is your home!" Home is a person.

"These objects were the treasures that made the condo feel like home."

More people are living alone in our world than ever. There is a loneliness epidemic on this crowded planet. Many people have the means to live alone instead of with all those difficult people who use their toothbrush, borrow their stuff, and don't wipe their feet, but maybe it is better to make a home with a difficult person than to live alone.

The United States Centers for Disease Control and the World Health Organization both warn that loneliness is bad for your health. Science shows that social isolation has a big effect on physical health, longevity, mental health, and quality of life. It has a similar impact to smoking, obesity, and a sedentary lifestyle. Loneliness puts people at greater risk of dementia, heart disease, and stroke. It actually shortens people's lives.

Whoa! I realize that the last paragraph was pretty gloomy. But anyone reading this who is *home* to others by inviting people for dinner, staying in touch with distant friends and relatives, celebrating birthdays, or greeting the clerk at the neighborhood store with a smile: kudos to you! The health warning is a nice exhortation when it is tempting to be too busy to connect with the people in our lives.

By living with others in a community, we learn to respect differences and dissolve our sense of separateness, which can make us feel isolated and unwanted. But, does that mean that no one who lives with others is ever lonely or someone who lives alone is lonely? Not necessarily, but being with others and having people in our hearts is essential to a sense of home.

My mom knew this. Her condo was home because of the relationships she had with the people in her heart. Even though some of her loved ones were gone, she felt close to them when she looked at the furnishings she had shared with them in her homes over the years. My dad and her mom, who she told us visited her every day, were her dear friends, the people who made her feel at home in this world and in the next.

Home Again Moment

Maybe it belongs—or belonged—to your spouse, child, aunt, uncle, etc., or a dear friend. Whenever you see or touch it, you feel at *home*, at ease, warm inside. That's what certain people feel like to us, even when they're not physically with us. It's not that *thing* you saw or touched. It's *them*. Think about the people who are not with you physically but in your heart and important to your sense of home.

Home Again Questions

What stood out, struck you, or moved you in this chapter?

This chapter reminds us, "Being with others and having people in our hearts is essential to a sense of home." Who is in your heart? Who is *home* to you? What are some ways you experience closeness to them in the place you call home?

For Further Reflection

Sometimes, the people who bring hominess into our lives are only an email, text message, or phone call away. Maybe we are home to *them* too. In what ways have you been *home* to others? Or, how can you bring a sense of hominess to someone else?

19

Home Is a Hideaway

I love hearing children shout out names as they hunt for a hiding kid. At our house and yard, they can't be found because the hiding places are just too good. But I also love to have the quiet in our home that comes when grown-ups and kids can hide in our house to be alone with their thoughts, a toy, a game, or a book. When our family writes articles, draws comics, designs curriculum, does math, meditates, or prays, we need places to hide.

When I took Elaine Aron's HSP (highly sensitive person) test, I discovered that I am in the 20% of people and animals that are more sensitive than average to all kinds of stimuli. She is a researcher who coined this term in the 1990s when she and her colleagues did extensive, fascinating research on the sensitivity of humans and many species of animals. She had been comforted by a therapist who gave her insights into her life by telling her to accept that she was a "highly sensitive person." I found it a bit of a relief to know that it is not shameful to be highly sensitive.

Being sensitive to my students, my family, or the poignant beauty of music or art can be an asset, even though it comes with being overwhelmed and overstimulated at times. So I sometimes get jangled by the noise and hubbub of life, even though I love the adventure of taking the wondrous opportunities of living and love. When I have been to a wedding, out to a community event, or taught a class full of eager students, I need to come home to a *place of repose*. I need to quiet my revving engine and process all the myriad of sights, sounds, and ideas swirling in my day. Of course, this is true for all humans; it just happens more often to the people in that 20% of the bell-shaped curve that Elaine Aron discovered.

I was inspired by a mother who gave advice on raising sensitive kids, who said she always allowed kids to hide away in the house as much as they wanted. The only rule was that when she called, they had to come out of hiding. I think it's helpful for a family if the parent can say, "You may find me hiding away in my bedroom when I need to. Just knock on the door if you need me."

When I show friends around our little bungalow on the East Hill of Eau Claire, I explain that our home does not have the popular "open plan" but a closed plan. We walk through the small havens of coziness made by the ability to close the heavy (somewhat dinged-up) polished wood doors that divide the small rooms from each other. Smaller spaces are easier to make cozy. For example, I don't mind the lack of square footage in our galley kitchen when I close the heavy wood doors and chop and sauté onions and garlic while listening to Rachmaninoff. It's nice to know that the coziness of the conversation by the fire on the other side of the door is not disturbed by those who may not care for the Romantic Russian composer in my kitchen hideaway.

Yesterday, we sunned ourselves on the little warm glassed-in front porch with cushioned seats and a sunny southern exposure view of our snowy neighborhood. On the north side of the house, my husband drinks his morning coffee and meditates in "The Cozy Room." This small room has a teal braided rug, a matching old wicker rocker, a beautiful gas fireplace, and seven windows with a view of the eastern sky's sunrise and backyard birds. In the laundry room, children like to hide in the low triangular-shaped alcove under the stairs next to a quilted bed with its cozy light (yes, we have a *guest bed* in our laundry room, just like in the movie *Dan in Real Life*). I was able to hide away quietly in that bed many nights, so I would not wake anyone during frequent late calls when my mother was dying. It is a great private space if you don't mind people coming in to move their clothes to the dryer.

"In my experience, people do not lead lives of unremitting 'quiet desperation' but are secretly connected, in their hidden moments of grace, to inspirations of comfort and joy."

I don't want to forget the outdoor hideaways. We often retreat to our screened-in pavilion for a quiet lunch. We enjoy lying in the rope hammock in the private side yard and watching the pine tree that fills the sky, swaying in the wind. Lounging there when I was delirious from COVID, I was comforted by the singing and talking of five species of birds in the mulberry tree and noisy meetups of a few families of squirrels and bunnies. I listen to the rain on the metal roof of the shed, from its comfy wicker chairs, and watch the raindrop races on the shed windows. The shed also serves as a nice private phone booth.

In my experience, people do not lead lives of unremitting "quiet desperation" but are secretly connected, in their hidden moments of grace, to inspirations of comfort and joy. When I am exhausted from cooking and dishes, I take solitary walks in the nearby woods, stand and survey our neighborhood from the hill, or retreat to the coffee shop down the hill. Sometimes, I light a candle in our neighborhood church or sit in the cozy nooks of the church library. Hidden, I look at God and God looks at me. I find invisible treasures of stillness and sacredness to carefully carry home.

Home Again Moment

It is good for us humans to be *with* others so we don't fall into loneliness, but we also have the need to be alone. Sometimes, we need this in our own houses. The Beach Boys recorded a song called, "In My Room." It expresses the sense of security and privacy that being alone in one's own space brings. A space in which we daydream and plan. A space that is a *home* within a home.

Home Again Questions

What stood out, struck you, or moved you in this chapter?

At home, there are times we are up and doing, and other times we want to retreat or go into a "hideaway." Do you have a hideaway in your house? What do you do there, and how do you feel when you are there?

For Further Reflection

There's a difference between being *alone* and being *lonely*. Some people *like* alone time, but maybe no one likes being *lonely*.

This might reflect how *you* feel. You occasionally (maybe regularly) like or *need* time to yourself and for yourself. And maybe this sometimes is true of how a friend or family member feels. How good it is to have and give others *space* to be alone!

20

Home Is a Hidden Art Gallery

This is what I looked like when I played
basketball with monks in the 1950s.

I learned about hidden art when I was a fourth grader, and my brother and I played basketball with monks. A bunch of us Catholic grade schoolers often had lessons on dribbling, passing, and free throws on Saturdays in the Holy Cross school gym. The monks managed to do this while still wearing their long brown robes tied with a rope at the waist. During basketball time, a monk would gently invite kids to an optional time of Franciscan teaching in a classroom. I was among the few kids who would choose that over learning the art of free throws. I needed an escape from basket-balling, an activity that highlighted the downside of the otherwise prized distinction of being the smallest girl in my class. (I weighed 45 pounds in fourth grade, which is what the average first grader weighs.)

Anyway, I and a handful of little people sat in short blond classroom chairs while a cheery young monk wearing a brown robe drew concentric circles on the blackboard with white chalk. This was something new. I expected him to be like the strict nun who called on us to recite the Baltimore Catechism in religion class. His smile lines deepened, and his eyes shone as he pointed to these circles and told us of the all-encompassing love of God going out in waves to all creation.

Of all the art I had seen on the chalkboards and bulletin boards and all the words I had heard explaining God in the school, his drawings and words were the most creative and emotion-filled to me. He was expressing the hidden beauty in his heart. I wish the scene had been filmed, but it was one of the millions of hidden works of art that happen every day. If someone was filming me listening to him, it would have been of an awe-struck little girl with chin-length straight, brown hair (unless I slept in curlers), and short bangs, whose feet did not touch the floor. To portray the inner workings of my heart, the film should be of me with a sea wind blowing in my hair, a golden light on my face, and Handel's *Water Music* playing in the background. He explained that even children could follow St. Francis of Assisi, and he passed out sweet-smelling mimeographed sheets with light blue print (remember those?) with a little temporary children's vow and some prayers for children, called an "office." Mesmerized, I made the vow and started to pray the "office" every day.

Even a year later, I would kneel every morning alone in my pink, lacy, sunlit bedroom and pray the Franciscan prayer before biking off to school in my white blouse, green plaid school jumper, white anklets, and brown tie shoes. That prayer goes like this: "May I not so much seek to be understood as to understand, to be consoled as to console." Hmm. Even as a fifth grader, I had the deeply uncomfortable realization that I was praying against my own self-interest. I was a kid who was very aware that I wanted to be understood, consoled, and loved more than I wanted to understand, console, and love others—especially at home. Here I was, every morning, quietly in my room, kneeling and praying that I would become the opposite of my natural self. This prayer felt unnatural. The art of homemaking is a little unnatural, too, in that it often quietly puts others' interests above self-interest.

For example, Mother Teresa sacrificed her sleep. While others slept, she had some quiet time to type letters to people she didn't even know, like us. This is how she ended her letter on March 13, 1985, addressed to us: "Never let anything so fill you with sorrow as to make you forget the joy of the risen Christ." It hangs on our dining room wall. The letter to us was mailed from Calcutta to Eau Claire, Wisconsin, signed by Mother Teresa. It was typed on an old typewriter that needed the ribbon changed. Hidden away in her room early in the morning, she would express the beauty of her soul as she typed. Her letter is one of the millions of hidden works of art created every day.

Mother Teresa exemplifies to me the art of homemaking in small, hidden ways in her homes for the dying and her homes for orphans. She creatively and beautifully made an art out of doing the smallest acts with a lot of love. Mother Teresa is famous not just for doing something beautiful for God in her homes for the dying but for her words to each of us about *our* homes.

She told us that if you want to bring happiness to the entire world, be loving in your family and home. She taught us that what you do for your family, you do for God. She also reminded us that loving people far away is easier than those close at hand. It is best to start by loving those close to us in our homes.

In the 1970s, a friend and Eau Claire nursing colleague of mine, Randi Johnson, traveled to a community in Taizé, France, from Madison, Wisconsin, where we were in nursing school together. She was surprised to find that Mother Teresa was there, too, visiting the same community. Instead of giving a public speech to the many people who wanted to see her, she arranged to greet each person quietly and individually. Mother Teresa had an intimate interaction with each person, known only to that person and hidden from everyone else. They formed a long line, and Randi said, "Mother Teresa silently greeted each of us by grasping our hands and lovingly gazing into our eyes. I feel in hindsight that I think perhaps she imparted to me the ability to see the good in everyone." Mother Teresa imparted a hidden art to Randi that, in later years, brought beauty to Randi's home and beyond.

"Ordinary lives may at first seem, well, ordinary, but if we look closely, we can see the distinct beauty of each individual that makes our homes into hidden art galleries."

Regarding this, we were a bit surprised a few years ago when a film crew requested to come to our little East Hill bungalow to interview us about Randi and her husband's hidden art in their Eau Claire home—since we are some of the few people who know about their quiet mission that is touching the homes of many across the world. This story is told in a documentary about Randi and her husband Brian, *Mom & Dad's Nipple Factory*—an art gallery that would have stayed hidden if their son, Justin, had not been a filmmaker. It's about Randi and Brian's journey of suffering and ingenuity that turned their breast cancer experience into a hidden art and a spare bedroom in their home into a Nipple Factory—a gift to the underserved women who have a need for beautiful prosthetic nipples after breast cancer surgery to compassionately restore beauty, dignity, and wholeness.

In our neighborhood church, we just celebrated people whose lives are hidden works of art, All Souls' Day, which is two days after "All Hallows' Eve" (AKA Halloween). On this day we remember the hidden works of art of those no longer with us. It is celebrated in the beginning of November by people all over the world in beautiful, culturally diverse ways, such as Mexico's Dia de los Muertos, Guatemala's Giant Kite Festival, and Poland's Feast of Bonfires and Candles, to name a few. It is cool to think that this holiday has been celebrated for over a thousand years in countries all over the globe. In many countries, this is a public holiday where people get off work so they can celebrate with their families with traditional foods and trips to church or the cemetery. On this special day, we go beyond celebrating the famous big saints and celebrate the throng of all the hidden saints and hallowed souls in our midst, living and dead, who have made their homes into hidden art galleries of love by serving each other in practical ways.

People all over the world are doing small, hidden, creative Works of Mercy in their homes because of their desire to do something beautiful and to strengthen the love in their homes. We have a list of the ancient "Works of Mercy" haphazardly posted on our laundry room cupboard door on pink paper. Simply said, it is a list of practical ways to do good to our fellow human beings that dates back to antiquity and has inspired famous artists for centuries. The Works of Mercy have been the subject of classic art, such as Caravaggio's painting from the 1600s, which still hangs in Naples for tourists to see. They have also been adapted for the theater by the Royal Shakespeare Company. So, tacking them up in our basement laundry room may be a little like slapping a Rembrandt painting on the side of a truck, but in my defense, I posted that list to remind us of the hidden art of homemaking we want to have in *our* home.

When I am daydreaming while I'm folding laundry and look up and see the list, it helps me to notice the hidden art of homemaking that happens in our homes. One thing on the list is "feed the hungry." My son brings this art to our home by frequently inviting a wide variety of people into our bungalow on the East Hill to eat his great Italian cooking, like great-grandma's meatballs, and his Korean food, like Budae-jjigae, also known as U.S. Army Soup. This comforting soup, a favorite of my grandchild (who has Korean taste buds), was invented in the 1950s to respond to starvation at the end of the Korean War. It was the result of large, homey potlucks between the U.S. Army and the war-weary South Koreans (who stood in soup lines). It is made of American processed meats such as chopped hot dogs or Spam, ramen noodles, kimchi, and any veggies around. Fortunately, we have a round table that always seems to have room for one more chair since the arrival of one more hungry guest than we expected is part of the fun.

Another Work of Mercy is to "visit the sick." We really have felt the importance of this work that came as a gift from our Eau Claire neighbors to our home recently since we have all had COVID. The many meals and offers of running to the store for us and other comforts (that make being very sick not so frightening) form concentric circles of love coming from our neighbors and friends. Once, when my husband had hip surgery, and I was exhausted, 13 people brought us delicious meals—unsolicited.

My daughter exemplifies the "shelter people" Work of Mercy by artistically designing a comfortable yet beautiful house and opening her doors to lots of people, from little people sleep-overs to large groups of people for parties, to people needing a place to stay. In the last year, she took in her cousin, who needed a place to live and work. She made room in her home and gave him a job in her business. Every room in the house is a work of art and comfort.

My husband is the person in the world who most exemplifies the Works of Mercy to me—the art of homemaking that brings comfort to the soul. When I am doubtful, confused, or have a selfish attitude, he sits down and gives me his ear. He prayerfully and patiently listens and creatively helps me solve my problems.

Everywhere and in every person, we can see this unique hidden art. Ordinary lives may at first seem, well, ordinary, but if we look closely, we can see the distinct beauty of each individual that makes our homes into hidden art galleries.

Home Again Moment

Many years ago, my husband was with our daughter in a very small California town for its Fourth of July parade on a beautiful sunny day. At a certain point, things became very still, and then, from a location he could not see, he heard children's voices begin to sing. They were singing the "Star Spangled Banner" a cappella, and to him, it sounded *magical* and *beautiful*. To him, it was a stunning piece of art heard by no one except those who had turned out for this parade in this tiny town. And, maybe, it was not considered *magical*, *beautiful*, or *art* by everyone there, but it was to my husband. Its deep beauty was hidden from much of the world. He savors the memory of this hidden art even today.

Home Again Questions

What stood out, struck you, or moved you in this chapter?

Think back to a time or situation in which you saw, heard, or experienced something very beautiful to *you*, even if relatively few others did. How long ago was it? What did it feel like to you then? What does it feel like to you today?

For Further Reflection

Do you recall a time when you created "hidden" art for someone else to enjoy? Describe what you did. If you can't recall such a time, what are some ways you can create or share something beautiful with someone else?

21

Home Is a Story We Find Ourselves In

In the 1940s, during Partition, little Muslim children migrating to Pakistan and little Hindu children migrating south to India had something in common. They both loved J. M. Barrie's story of *Peter Pan*, who recruited the little homemaker, Wendy, to go to Neverland to nurture the "lost boys" who had lost their homes when they fell out of their baby buggies. In the '30s and '40s, when Stalin sent over three million people to Siberia as slave labor, schoolchildren in Siberia were reading about how slavery tore families apart in *Uncle Tom's Cabin* by Harriet Beecher Stowe. People all over the world are interested in stories of losing a home and finding it again because that is the human story. And stories full of the little things that make a home precious renew our ability to see how to make a home.

In the snow, my children and the neighbor kids would put on their parkas, mittens, and boots and walk past the Uniroyal Tire Factory, down the hill by the Eau Claire River, past Poo Corner (the old mansion on the corner with lots of dog mess), to the L. E. Phillips Public Library.

We carried home mounds of books in our backpacks—tales for the imagination. We would enter the homes of the Berenstain Bears family, the Ingalls family's *Little House on the Prairie*, and the Seven Dwarfs' cozy home in the woods.

When my imagination brings me into the homemaking descriptions of Kenneth Grahame about Mole and Ratty's hospitality to the Christmas caroling mice in *The Wind in the Willows*, or Madeleine L'Engle's homemaking narrative of 5-year-old Charles Wallace's sandwich-making, I feel I am in their homes, like I'm transported into a story very different from my regular life.

I want to serve supper, hot drinks, and savory comforts to people coming in from the cold, like Mole and Ratty in the Christmas chapter.

I feel like I, too, am sheltered in the farmhouse kitchen on a "dark and stormy night" with Charles Wallace, of *A Wrinkle in Time* fame, making a liverwurst and cream cheese sandwich and hot cocoa—not just for his mother, but for me. I want to be like Mrs. Wallace, Charles' scientist mother who makes Boeuf Bourguignon on a Bunsen burner in her laboratory attached to the old farmhouse, or like Charles' teenage sister Meg who, in L'Engle's book, *A Ring of Endless Light*, makes Poor Man's Stroganoff when the family comes home from the hospital with their dying grandpa.

Even I can heat up some apple cider and put in a cinnamon stick or improvise a quick Poor Man's Stroganoff by taking some cream of mushroom soup, yogurt, ground beef, chopped onion, and mushrooms and serving it over hot rice. Judging by the seconds and thirds people dish up, this is better than it sounds.

I don't have a Bunsen burner, but I have made L'Engle-inspired Boeuf Bourguignon in the crock pot many times. This family favorite (otherwise known as beef stew) is made exquisite with two cups of le vin rouge (otherwise known as red wine).

I love picturing Peggotty, David Copperfield, and his mother sitting in the "parlor" in the evening after Peggotty's housekeeping work is done, just enjoying companionship. Dickens created a scene where David's mother, on a Sunday evening, makes the mistake of reading to David and Peggotty the story of Lazarus being raised from the dead by Jesus. This backfires. Dead people coming out of their graves is not a good bedtime story. That evening, little David is so frightened they have to show him the quiet churchyard cemetery out his window, where all the dead are lying in their graves, resting under the solemn moon. This comforts me in the midst of all the well-intentioned, memorable backfires of homemaking.

Cheryl Mendelson, a Harvard Law School graduate, sometime philosophy professor, and famed *New York Times* bestselling author of *Home Comforts: The Art and Science of Keeping House*, has captured my imagination. Not by motivating me to take her encyclopedia-like advice on the details of doing laundry or the correct way to hold a broom, but by her simple ideas that a bowl of fruit on the table, a little tidying, or having get-away spaces in the house make it cozy. She has done Americans the favor of making homemaking seem cool, interesting, and funny. Thank you, Cheryl, for reminding us that hoodies need to be laundered. Who knew?

Sometimes I wonder, like the hobbits in The Lord of the Rings, if I've been moved into a story very different than my usually comfortable, predictable life.

When my life starts to feel like a TV miniseries, the best story I know is the book by Darlene Deibler Rose, *Evidence Not Seen*, about homemaking while going through hell. This book is about her experience in New Guinea, in her 20s, as a Japanese prisoner during World War II. The violent Japanese commander put Darlene in charge of this half-block-long cement barrack of bamboo bunks to keep order and fulfill work assignments.

She brought her Midwest neighborly, compassionate values and organizational homemaking skills to the concentration camp. Barrack 8 became a calm center in the midst of the concentration camp, where families from other barracks came to join them for prayer at 7 p.m. Harmony reigned in Barrack 8. As soon as a vacancy was posted, inmates applied to take a spot there.

In Barrack 8, women who had been gourmet cooks in their pre-war lives knew how to make the old coffee grounds taste like fresh coffee. Women who had physical strength would take the harder work duties to spare the elderly. Grandmothers took care of the young children, and nursing mothers nursed other women's babies when the mothers were too ill. When a young girl, Dolly, became paralyzed from the waist down by meningitis, everyone in the barrack helped her learn to walk again, using the ladders of the top sleeping racks to brace herself.

This Midwest newlywed, whose husband died in the nearby men's camp, inspired an interracial, interfaith group of women to overcome language barriers and make Barrack 8 into a home that enabled each of them to face suffering, hunger, deprivation of every kind, forced labor, bombings, disease, psychological pressures, death, and lonely graves.

"People all over the world are interested in stories of losing a home and finding it again because that is the human story."

Identifying with the stories of others, whether a hero like Darlene or an everyman character like Mole in *The Wind in the Willows*, helps us see that we are in a story, too. When Sam, the hobbit, in *The Two*

Towers, acknowledges that he and Frodo have found themselves in a story very different than their usually comfortable and predictable life, it is an acknowledgment that we don't often plan our adventures, but we find ourselves in them and don't know how they will end. We don't know if our adventures in homemaking will end with us as the hero meeting the needs of others or the needy person who finds a home from the generosity of others.

But we do know that telling our stories, especially in rich narratives with the complexity of emotions and history, along with light and positivity, has a health-giving effect. We learn this from the brains of a bunch of ordinary Minnesota nuns who lived together, teaching school, cooking meals, eating and celebrating holidays together, doing crafts, and choral singing in harmony. Please bear with me as I gush a little about brain research. (It's an occupational hazard of a nerdy passionate science teacher.) The Nun Study follows the lives of 180 School Sisters of Notre Dame living in Mankato, Minnesota, looking at the connection between their handwritten autobiographies, their health, and their brains.

These teaching nuns, who lived together in a homey community, donated their journals and their skulls (post-mortem, of course) to science so they could continue teaching after they were gone. Yes, their carefully labeled brains are now residing at the University of Minnesota just across the St. Croix River, not far from here. It is so cool that even though the nuns are no longer with us, they teach us that certain kinds of telling of our tale can be medicinal. Storytelling can help us age with grace. A great deal of protection from dementia in the nuns was correlated with optimistic storytelling and richer vocabulary. How you tell the tale of your life affects your level of happiness and longevity.

Getting children, teens, and young adults in our households or classrooms to tell their stories can be as important to their health as good nutrition—an important part of homemaking.

In the '90s, I stayed up late because I couldn't be in a hurry to find out how my teens' days went. Sadly, 10 p.m. seemed to be the golden hour when they were ready to speak. Our back-door neighbor told me that she would wait until the opportune moment and call her various teens on the upstairs phone that rang from the downstairs phone. They were often only ready to speak about their day on the telephone. One teen we know seems to like to tell the stories of his day only after a snack, a game of WORDLE, or chess. The unfolding of these rich tales in our homes can't be hurried, but waiting for the teller to speak is worth the wait.

Home Again Moment

Our day-to-day lives, or perhaps the larger trajectory of our lives, can sometimes feel like a tense plot line from a novel . . . or a movie with a story that is distressing and so complicated that even we have trouble following it! Like the hobbits in The Lord of the Rings, we wonder if we've somehow been moved into a story very different than our usually comfortable, predictable lives! But we can sometimes catch refreshing glimpses of others navigating the same or similar difficulties, which gives us hope that *we* will be OK in the end.

Home Again Questions

What stood out, struck you, or moved you in this chapter?

Try to recall a time in your life or a set of circumstances that made you feel like you were in a tense TV miniseries. What got you through that time? Was there another storyline you turned to for hope or inspiration? When I lived through difficult storylines, I derived a sense of hope and inspiration by recalling the "best story" I know: the true story of Darlene Deibler Rose, told in the book *Evidence Not Seen*. If you have to live through a difficult set of circumstances in the future, what stories do you know that could give you hope and inspiration?

For Further Reflection

The next time you feel like you're trapped in a tense TV miniseries, what would happen if you imagined how it could turn out with you not only being okay but *stronger*? Perhaps practice this kind of outlook with less tense situations so you'll be better prepared.

22

Home Is a Science Experiment

When I was 7, I practiced spelling by insulting my smiley, blond 2-year-old sister, who had not yet heard of the alphabet. When she did not share a Tinker Toy or Lincoln Log or commit any other great offense, I called her a P-I-G-G-Y or B-A-B-B-Y. Sometimes, I hurled insults at this oblivious, giggly toddler higher than her vocabulary without spelling them since "disobedient" or "selfish" were harder for me to spell. When I tried this with my older 8-year-old brother, high conflict with a much more skilled speller would ensue. My parents, even though they didn't know the scientific nature of their exhortation, made me apologize and learn to say nice things to my siblings, to share, and to be kind. For the most part, peace was regained again and again because of this insistence on saying nice things.

There *is* science behind this. Doctors in love, Julie and John Gottman (a happily married scientist couple) started a science experiment about the happiness of homes called *The Love Lab* at the University of

Washington. From them, we know that a happy home needs five positive interactions to every negative one. So the one nasty name-calling, such as B-A-B-B-Y, needs five kindnesses to make up for it.

"Did you argue when you were little?" While my husband and I and our four grade school-age grandchildren were sitting around the table, the almost first grader brought this subject up. Funny, you should ask . . . "Yes." Actually, I spared her the famous story of when I was in grade school, and I ended an argument by flipping the Monopoly board and flouncing out in a rage. From my grandma perspective, my grandkids had nothing to worry about. They had the Gottman five-to-one ratio down. An older sibling often ran to the aid of a younger sibling who had gotten into a jam, such as up a tree, and couldn't get down. The two older girls took turns comforting a crying younger one, frightened at the top of a slide or waking up on the wrong side of the bed. "I got this," said the oldest as she ran to the aid of her toddler brother, who had just been hit by a little girl at a mall play area.

I watched their mom, who fostered this kindness between her children by giving the older ones the job of packing backpacks and helping the younger ones get ready for outings. The little one who had asked, "Did you argue…?" often set up her even younger brother with a drink and snack on the couch before watching a cartoon together. She said to him, "I always get you situated." The boy, who was born on St. Patrick's Day, took on the job of making his three older sisters laugh with shenanigans and malarky—such as telling wild stories about monsters and moon trips or soft-shoeing a top hat and cane routine. He had to pause the act to breathe because he was laughing so hard.

☼☼☼

In the early 2000s, when I was in my 50s and launching kids into college, I took a pathophysiology class at UW–Eau Claire just to see if

I liked the process of learning. I also wanted to be sure my own life, not my kids' lives, flashed before me when I died. I was fascinated by the new research (at least new to me) since my last pathophysiology class was in the '70s. We were asked to pick a chapter in our textbook and do a written and oral report on the research. I chose the chapter on the science of psychoneuroimmunology—the new field of research about the connection between the mind and the body. I read that mindfulness meditation can help our bodies and our homes.

This led me to do more study of the research on mindfulness meditation, practice it at home, and pass it on to my patients. The most rewarding thing was seeing what the science experiment of mindfulness was doing to change my patients' homes.

"This little window meditation, practiced consistently, had brought her back from the land of terror to her children."

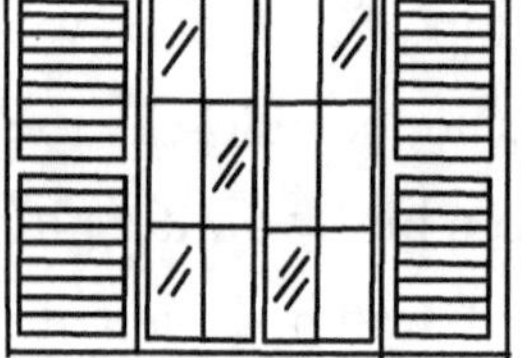

When my patient Dakota's 19-year-old son was deployed to the Middle East, she was so panicky that she practically forgot she had three other children, even though one preschooler was home with her the whole day. She lay awake at night, gripped with pictures of combat. She avoided listening to news reports, but in her head, she was terrorized. Other parents all over the globe whose kids were deployed were struggling with this, but since she had a mood disorder, she was questioning her hope of surviving.

Dakota arrived at my private practice "home" on Barstow Street in Eau Claire in blue jeans and a cardigan, with combed hair and a friendly smile. She outwardly appeared to be a woman on solid footing, though she described an inner landscape in which she was clearly struggling with extreme emotions.

She was lost somewhere in her head and knew her other children really needed her to be with them now, but she had gone to terror land and did not know the way back. I suggested a form of walking meditation that included her 4-year-old girl, Kateri. She did this 6 days a week. For 30 minutes, usually after the older ones had gone to school, she and little Kateri would walk from window to window and examine with three senses what they heard, saw, and smelled.

Dakota smiled as she reported her progress to me during a follow-up visit to my office. Kateri thrived on the attention. She would talk about the sound of the birds outside the window and tell her about the rumble of the trucks or how the breeze felt. Dakota noticed what Kateri was noticing. This little window meditation, practiced consistently, had brought her back from the land of terror to her children. It had shown her the way to gently escort her mind to the present.

When I taught the psychiatric nursing class for undergraduates at UW–Eau Claire, I asked each of my students to do a science experiment in their home. I presented them with research about a myriad of positive psychology interventions like gratitude, exercise, how food affects mood, getting out in nature, laughter, forgiveness, meditation (of course), journaling, and prayer, to name a few. Then, they chose an activity that tickled their fancy to do for 2 weeks and journaled the comparison between how they felt before and after. The students wrote about significant transformations in their feelings and perspectives and how roommates and family members noticed a big positive difference in them. Almost every science experiment essay concluded with a commitment.

"I'm going to keep watching funny videos with friends every day."

"My family and I are changing the way we eat forever . . . we feel so good."

"Running is going to be part of my life from now on."

"I plan to keep using a meditation app every morning when I wake up."

Experimenting with the Science of Positive Psychology, which is full of seeds of happiness, can change our lives and our homes.

Home Again Moment

I was able to observe my daughter foster the five-to-one kindness ratio with her four school-age children. Sometimes we can improve a relationship skill by watching others live it. Is there a person or a family in your life that does well at the five-to-one kindness ratio?

Home Again Questions

What stood out, struck you, or moved you in this chapter?

Sometimes our five-to-one ratio gets out of whack. Maybe more often with a specific person than with just anyone. How can we keep our five-to-one more in place with *this* person?

For Further Reflection

How did the story about Dakota in the chapter affect you? Have you ever been willing, like Dakota, to try something that *might* bring you more peace or strength? Is there something in your life (perhaps less troubling than Dakota's challenge) that mindfulness or some other practice could help you with?

23

Home Is a Playground

"Red Rover, Red Rover, send Robbie right over," was my team's cry as we, a long snake of 6-year-olds fiercely holding hands, stood opposite the other team of a long snake of children holding hands.

Then Robbie, running full blast at us, would try to pick the weakest link of hands to break through and get the reward of taking one of our kids back to join their team. Then *they* shouted the "Red Rover" to dare one of us, and we would send our teammate to try to break through and hopefully bring us a kid back. It had the thrill of tackle football one collision at a time and has been known to send children to the hospital.

And then there was *Crack the Whip*, a game in which the leader of a long snake of children would run swerving wildly to toss off the kid at the end of the line. A game whose end goal seemed to result in laughs, skinned knees, and band-aids handed out by the teacher.

Other more artistically inclined 6-year-olds were drawing large animals, such as birds with 5-foot wingspans and life-size donkeys, in the sand with sticks that had fallen from the bowering oak trees that shaded our playground sandlot. We were careful not to step on them. After a half hour on the sandlot, the mid-morning bell would ring, and we filed in and sat at our assigned first-grade desks.

After recess, I was homesick when I sat at my little blond desk in the fall of 1957. But that feeling disappeared again after lunch when the real reason to go to school resumed: recess. I only felt at home when we were on the playground.

The playground at Holy Cross School in Champaign would resound with that familiar, loud sound that is known to all people who live near a grade school and are accustomed to the triumphant noise that comes from the "outdoor" voices of hundreds of kids in various states of raucous play. After sitting at our desks with our feet on the floor since the bus or our mothers dropped us off in the morning, we would "get the wiggles out" with very little supervision.

Yes, there was the trading game the nuns would probably not have sanctioned. We brought the baseball cards that we got in bubble gum packs and traded them for cards the nuns gave out as prizes. Like, "I'll trade you a Mickey Mantle for a Therese the Little Flower." That trade would have been a hard decision for me since I collected all things Yankee and St. Therese was my favorite.

By second grade, a much more illicit activity was happening on the playground: the passing of love notes. At lunch recess, I had the humiliating experience of receiving one of these greasy, wrinkled missives printed in No. 2 pencil. I was quietly reading it after recess at my little desk in the back of the third aisle of desks when, to my shock, a tiny girl named Shirley raised her hand and tattled that I was reading a love note. This revelation resulted in my walk of shame to the front of the class, where I had to hand it over to the shocked teacher. I completely agreed with the kindly but bewildered nun in her disapproval of the playground practice, especially because it was from "That Gary." Couldn't it have been from the other Gary, so at least the long walk to the front of the class would have been a thrilling walk of a romantic nature, well worth the blushing?!

To give a little history, that playground note was from the same blond crew-cutted, round-faced, cherub-cheeked Gary who had called my home to declare his love. I don't remember how the phone call went, but my mother often told of the conversation with a laugh. I, lacking the tact to graciously reject his hopeful advances, slammed the classic old-style black phone down on its receiver, ending the short conversation with the salvo, "That is the problem! You love me, but I don't love you!"

Eventually, at the end of that embarrassing school day, we rode the bus home, and after graham crackers and milk and complaining about my love note mortification to my mother, I played some more with my siblings and the neighbor kids in my yard, which amounted to a mini-playground.

In the backyard of the aforementioned little green house, with the aforementioned septic tank, we had a rather large "playhouse." I think we inherited it from the previous owner, who used it as a doghouse for some rather large dogs. It had a grown-up human-size and a dog-size entrance. We "slept" on the shelves that we imagined into bunk beds and ate "mud pies" at a little table, and hid from the fierce warrior boys who shot rubber, suction-cup-tipped arrows from their bows at the playhouse. We stayed away from the window with its fluttering curtain to avoid being "dead." It felt especially exciting because we could see daylight through the holes in the wood of the playhouse from the previous arrow and BB gun shooting. Activities my mother put a quash on unless the playhouse was unoccupied and a bull's eye was set up. With all the goings on with my brother's Crabby Appleton Club initiation requirement of eating a worm and the finding of dirty baby birds that had fallen out of nests, my mom had to have eyes in the back of her head.

Usually, we were just peacefully imitating the work our parents did in real life by playing house. We had cast-off dishes and silverware that kept migrating to the sandbox, where we prepared the savory "poison berry" sand pies. We also caught bugs in jars for pets, inhabited the swing set with vigor, teeter-tottered recklessly, and slid down the slide into the dirt. We sometimes had to do real work in the backyard, like sweep the sidewalk or pick the fruits from the garden. We made play of our work and work of our play.

Naturally, as I grew into a teen in the 1960s in Winchester, Massachusetts, I felt most at home in friends' houses when the family knew how to play. One of these homes was the home of a dearly beloved high school friend, Bob Shannon, who became a computer scientist. There was a fleet of unicycles there and assorted juggling clubs. A chair lift and zip line ran down a big hill through the trees to the Mystic Lakes. There were all kinds of musical instruments and chess games and lots of fun contraptions made by Bob's famous mathematician parents. The conversation around the dinner table was light-hearted. It was said of his father, Claude Shannon, that he worked with levity and played with gravity. He never acknowledged the difference.

I didn't realize he was famous until my communication professor at the University of Wisconsin–Madison, in 1970, lectured on Mr. Shannon's contributions to the science of communication. Claude Shannon is remembered in the annals of the history of science as the "Father of the Information Age."

Before he lived in the house in Winchester, where he taught at nearby MIT, he taught at Princeton (at the same time as Albert Einstein). Earlier during WWII, Alan Turing was pulled off the Enigma code-breaking project in England and went to Washington D.C. to work under Shannon on the stressful work of scrambling the secure telephone conversations between Churchill and FDR. Shannon and Turing enjoyed lunch breaks together and discussed the interesting, hopeful math ideas that led to today's computers. Mr. Shannon said that the most fun he ever had was figuring out the connection between the ones and zeros of binary math, electrical switches, and formulas for the speed and accuracy of perfect communication, which started the race to build digital versus mechanical "thinking machines." Though he is not a household name, many believe this modest, playful dad of my friend was the most important scientist of our time; at least, he had the most famous master's thesis. He was even on a Google Doodle in 2016, picturing him on a unicycle juggling ones and zeros.

"Though he is not a household name, many believe this modest, playful dad of my friend was the most important scientist of our time . . ."

But his influence on me was from the home he created with an aura of play with a capital "P." Something in me relaxes when I think of their home with its view of the lake, tall library with a ladder to reach the upper books, and its room full of weaving looms. It helps me accept my own home as a unique and maybe even sometimes a bit quirky playground and not as a showcase of grim determination to be perfect. We need more fun in our work and more serious play, and Shannon's philosophy still teaches us the way.

Home Again Moment

I've heard playing described as doing something that is humorous, fun, or simply enjoyable in itself. Children in the home often spend a lot of time *playing*. Adults, not so much! What would your personal version of Claude Shannon's *working with levity and playing with gravity* look like? Is there any work that feels like play to you?

Home Again Questions

What stood out, struck you, or moved you in this chapter?

What is something *humorous, fun, or simply enjoyable in itself* that you could do either by yourself or with a friend or family member *this week*? What would you need to plan or do to make sure it happens? How often would you like this to happen? What's realistic?

For Further Reflection

Science has shown the health benefits of play for adults, and play is associated with higher creativity and appreciation of beauty. What kind of play brings out *your* creativity? What kind of play gets you in touch with beauty? How do you feel physically after playing?

THE WAY HOME

24

The Beatitude (Happiness) of Home Poverty

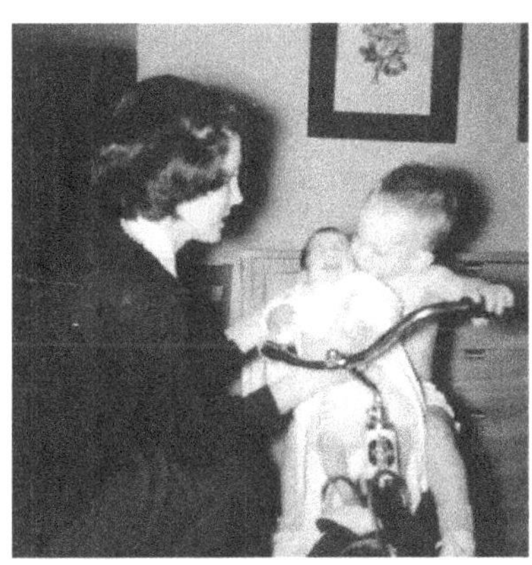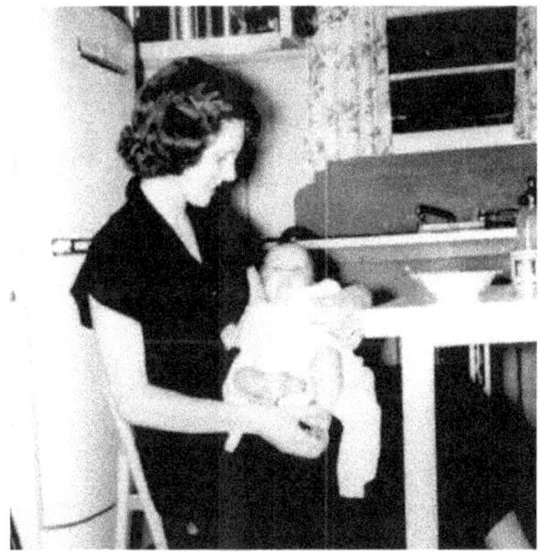

I was born into the happy home in remodeled army barracks. Seen here, held by my brother and my mom.

When my parents lived in a community of remodeled barracks by the railroad tracks in Champaign, Illinois, and my dad got a job in the university bursar's office after he graduated in accounting, my mom joined the University Wives Association. Their home was part of university married student housing, which they had moved into before my dad graduated. They barely had two nickels to rub together, but my mom did know how to entertain since her family had owned a nightclub next to their house. She had the ability to smile, laugh, and pour coffee with the best of them.

One afternoon, in the early '50s, she hosted part of the Wives club, including the president of the university's wife, Margaret Stoddard, in their cramped quarters for coffee and coffee cake. My brother, who was around 3 at the time, locked himself in the only bathroom. Since he was attracted to razors and shaving cream, it was pretty exciting. My understanding is that his hijinks included running himself a bath. Fun!

No one could get the door opened from the outside, and they couldn't get him to open the door or window, so they waited in a state of high drama for the university maintenance man to show up! Obviously, he had other priorities, so my brother was still happily messing around naked in the locked bathroom when people began to leave the coffee party. Part of the dilemma was the natural consequence of the consumption of lots of coffee and an occupied bathroom. When Margaret, the president's wife, left, she said to my mom, "What will you do if you can't get him out of there tonight?" My mom happily said (and I quote), "I guess I'll just have to have another one."

Fast forward a few years. My mother demonstrated a happy humility of spirit in her home when her guests exerted their superiority. For example, there was one couple (who was much more worldly and wealthy) who would come to visit and stay with them. They liked to actually rearrange my mother's furniture as if they were consultants whom she had called in to improve her interior decorating. These new floor plans were not improvements, in my opinion. I had recently read Miss Manners' column in the newspaper that covered the proper etiquette rules when guests behave in this way. So, I passed on Miss Manners' suggestion—if they think that is polite—then mom should rearrange their furniture when she visits their home. Miss Manners does give the caveat that she is only instructing in manners, not necessarily in charity. My mom wisely declined that suggestion. Smiling, she said, "This is their expertise that they are offering to me, and I am afraid that I will hurt their feelings if I rearrange it back too quickly."

Beatitude is one of those old words I love. It comes from Old French and just means a saying that teaches you how to be happy. Nevertheless, the beatitude, "Blessed are the poor in spirit, for theirs is the kingdom of heaven," really seemed confusing to me when I was in grade school. The first person I realized was poor was a little girl that I saw from the car window when my dad was parking our car before Sunday Mass at Holy Cross Church. I asked my mom, "Why is that little girl going into church wearing dirty shorts without her hair combed?" Mom said she was "poor." She didn't look happy, so when I heard that the poor in spirit were happy or blessed, I pondered it for years.

"My mother demonstrated a happy humility of spirit in her home when her guests exerted their superiority."

Of course, severe poverty is very sad. That is why our nursing department at UW–Eau Claire is involved in so many projects to help people who have no health care, such as delivering babies on a Native American reservation, working at the local Free Clinic, giving immunizations at Community Table in downtown Eau Claire, and providing free care to farm workers who have no insurance. I am happy I live in a neighborhood where a neighbor felt free to ask me if she could bring someone to my house to get some clothes for her office job out of my closet. She was an abused woman who had just left her home with only the clothes on her back and her children. The woman was the same size as me.

Today, even though severe poverty will always make us sad, the beatitude does teach me a happy idea. I feel happy when I realize that everyone who comes into my East Hill bungalow in Eau Claire, Wisconsin, is my superior in some way. I can be happy to host them even if I'm a poorer cook, gardener, or writer. It's OK that I don't have the stamina of young folks. I can be a receiver of other people's riches. It's OK that two of the people who came to visit our house this week made a meal to share with our family, knowing that Lou and I get pretty tuckered out. They can invite themselves over for a fun night that involves a great meal they brought rather than depending on our stamina, at ages 71 and 68, to spread the table. And a few more of the meals this week were made by my son and grandchild. I am blessed, indeed. I can be happy even though I keep getting weaker as I age and poorer in health and abilities because I am blessed.

Now I get it. "Blessed are the poor in spirit, for theirs is the kingdom of heaven."

Home Again Moment

After seeing that "poor" girl near our church (who certainly didn't look happy), *I pondered for years* the phrase from the Gospel, "Blessed are the poor in spirit." Sometimes, there might be an idea or perspective about life, other people, or ourselves that puzzles us. Maybe it takes us a long time to arrive at that moment where we say, "Ahhhh . . . *now* I see."

Home Again Questions

What stood out, struck you, or moved you in this chapter?

How would you react if guests in your home rearranged your furniture so it was "better?" Maybe something this extreme hasn't ever happened to you, but how do you respond when someone suggests a better way to do something or proposes a different way to view or think about something? Are you open to the idea that they are *right*? At least "right" enough for you to *consider* what they have said? Why, or why not?

If you consider their point of view and don't agree, how do you decide whether to stand up for yourself by making a clear-cut boundary or a tactful approach where you steer the ship through the rocks? How do you stay friends with people you don't agree with?

For Further Reflection

"Everyone who comes into my East Hill bungalow in Eau Claire, Wisconsin, is my superior in some way." If you thought of *everyone* else as being your superior in some way (whether or not you've discovered what it was yet), how might this change the way you interact with others? How might it change the way you see yourself?

25

Home Dew Point

I think I am allowed one scientific formula in this book, so I have a question for anyone who has gotten this far. Have you ever heard of Td = T - ((100-RH)/5)?

I have an old high school friend whose father was a local TV weatherman. I asked him to explain the mysteries of the dew point to me. He probably had that formula for dew point in his head when he was explaining it. It is one of those things I pretend to understand, and even after the explanation, I am still only pretending. I can't think in metric, and T stands for temperature in Celsius (which is un-American), and I can't even imagine RH, which stands for relative humidity. Relative to what?

I do know that this refreshing and renewing dew we walk through on spring mornings (that gets our sneakers wet and waters our raised beds and grass) has its own rules. For example, today, January 30, 2023, as I am writing, my weather app says that in Eau Claire, the dew point is -9 degrees. Go figure. I do know that dew drops don't want to gather where there is heat and wind. The temperature must fall. The wind must cease. The air comes to a point of coolness and rest. The air yields up those more or less invisible particles of moisture when there is stillness.

I like to walk in the cool stillness of my own yard in the early morning. The glistening drops on the grass that soak my feet are my teachers. Nature is a schoolbook. It declares a message and always has—rest. Maybe not absolute rest, but some time in the day, stillness is needed as much as nutrients and sunshine for our lives.

"The glistening drops on the grass that soak my feet are my teachers."

When I get sped up and heated up, I can have the effect of heating up and speeding up my homelife. While recently sitting at the dining room table, my husband, Lou, kidded me, "Easy there, tiger!" I needed to drop the temperature and get out of the wind for everyone's sake.

I can sit my little self down in a quiet corner of my bungalow or take a quiet walk in my beloved East Hill, but then there is the problem of my mind. Some people call this problem "monkey brain" for obvious reasons. I turn to the still-mind expert for help, the expert on cooling our heads, Eknath Easwaran.

He is the first person to teach a class on meditation at a U.S. university. He was a Fulbright Scholar from India, a Hindu raised in a Catholic School. A mentor of Henri Nouwen, the beloved priest who lived in a community of people with disabilities and who had taught at Harvard Divinity School for many years.

Easwaran tells a story about crossing to America from India, his first time by sea. He explains that the sea is a great equalizer. The mighty *and* the simple folk are all prone to seasickness.

On the first leg of his journey in the Mediterranean, he was one of the only people on board who was not throwing up into a little bag as the sea tossed the small passenger ship around. He sat looking at the watery scenery and meditating to counter the nausea. Then, on the long trip across the Atlantic on a much bigger ship, when storms were encountered, the ship did not toss from side to side, and seasickness was minimized. Easwaran asked one of the staff why the ship was not pitching about in a storm. The sailor explained to him that they had just put in something new: stabilizers. Ahh, stabilizers.

The Meditation that Easwaran teaches in his books and website is a home stabilizer. Even though he passed many years ago, he still speaks to us with a message that can cool down and refresh our homes.

It is the most simple way of meditating I have found. I simply focus on a passage from any tried and true, durable piece of wisdom. Short and easy to repeat. He suggests it be something time-tested from the wisdom of the ages. Then, I secure my mind to that one ancient thought by repeating it as I walk or sit. I like "Be still and know that I am God." People who may not be comfortable with God often connect with Julian of Norwich's famous words, "All will be well, all will be well, all manner of things will be well." Then there is always the Buddhist loving-kindness meditation, "May I be well. May I be at peace. May my heart remain open."

The main thing is to set up my mind to welcome the dew, to find that sweet spot—the home dew point. It requires turning down the temperature and heat in my mind to set myself up for dew drops, for the refreshing rest of the soul from which everything beautiful in my home grows.

Home Again Moment

We can find our homelife temperatures rising and our inner calm disrupted by worries, anger, or conflicts with others in or outside our homes. In the natural world, there are "rules" that govern how and when it's cool enough for the sparkling dew drops to appear. There are things that *must* be in place or happen in order for those little drops to appear. So, too, there are "rules" for what must happen before the "temperature" of our *homes* drops, fostering a refreshing, cool stillness.

Home Again Questions

What stood out, struck you, or moved you in this chapter?

When your body and mind are caught up in the "heat and wind" generated by an unpleasant or upsetting situation, who are the people, or what are the places, things, or activities that help you to turn down the temperature inside you, and set you up "to welcome the dew (to find that sweet spot), the home dew point?"

For Further Reflection

This chapter reminds us that the natural world "is a schoolbook. It declares a message and always has—rest." How might you find times to slow down, to downshift to a lower gear at least for a little while—every day?

26

Lightening up Our Homes

Christmas is over. I saved some Christmas cards to look at again next year—ones with photos and especially the ones that are not all "sugar plums." I have three of the yearly Christmas cards from the same little growing family. They now have three kids being juggled by the parents in the cover photo. The first card summarizes their year in fancy writing splashed above the picture, "We're still married." The next year says, "We got a new marriage therapist!" in a joyful scroll above their family photo. And this year, it is, "All our nannies quit!"

I love to read honest cards that are very convincing in which people have some legitimate complaints to be aired about their year while wishing us happy holidays. We sail along in life. Suddenly, a great storm sweeps down, washing away all, or most of, our peaceful feelings. Sometimes, I think that fewer of these storms would be beneficial to my peace of mind. When St. Teresa of Avila was knocked off her horse into the mud on her travels, she looked up to heaven and quipped, "Dear God, if this is how you treat your friends, it is no wonder you have so few of them." Sometimes, the best thing to do is laugh.

In 2020, on the first day we got our pandemic dog, a 1-year-old golden Labrador retriever named Sly, we had the now famous Catastrophic Canine Caper. It was February and very cold when we drove a couple of hours north of Eau Claire to an animal shelter to pick him up. After we brought him home, we went out to run an errand in the late afternoon while our son cooked dinner, leaving our fifth-grade grandchild mostly in charge of watching the new dog. We came home to 10 pounds of tiny morsels of expensive dog food spread across the mudroom, kitchen, dining room, and living room floors. We are still getting them out from under the 100-year-old upright piano 3 years later. It could have happened when any of us were with Sly on his first day. Sly lived his whole life in neglect or in a shelter. Not knowing how much supervision he required, we might have given him too much freedom at first.

We ate a tense supper cooked by hungry people whose feet were crunching on the random dog food morsels that defied sweeping. Around the dining room table, a family meeting took place to decide if Sly was a keeper. After a lot of yelling, a very distressed dinner guest in his worn jeans and t-shirt (a fifth-grade neighbor boy) abruptly stood up and took charge of the meeting. He was the only one with a vestige of sanity remaining. He had clearly had it with all the drama and was used to speaking his mind about all things "pet." He convinced us that this was the best dog he had ever met. He knew a lot of dogs, including grouchy pit bulls, and he eloquently assured us we would never find one as good as Sly (who didn't know any better). "He's just a dog. A good dog!"

Tears were shed when we parted.

Eventually, the absurdity of the whole evening was not lost on us. After a good night's sleep, a "Was that really us?" moment, and a good laugh at ourselves, we voted to keep Sly (which lasted until allergies made it impossible). But we had him long enough for many merry adventures with that comical dog. Even though tears were shed when we parted, we still chuckle when telling funny tales of our adventures with this dear pink-nosed golden Lab, especially goofy stories that involve his patience when puppies repeatedly ran underneath him and a difficult decision Sly had to make about retrieving his beloved purple football when it landed in a pile of poop. The retriever instinct won out over our whole family's chorus of "No, No, No!" When we could no longer keep him, he continued his antics in the home of the aforementioned neighbor boy, his sister, his mother, and three cats, and after a year, retired to a country home where he could frolic with other dogs and wag, smile, and chase around to his heart's content.

In 1908, G. K. Chesterton wrote, "Angels fly because they take themselves lightly." I love how my Aunt Mary took herself lightly even after her husband's funeral.

When my parents were getting in the car after my uncle's funeral, my aunt, who had just lost her dear husband and was afraid to lose my mother in a car accident on her long car ride back to New England, said very seriously, "Please drive carefully!" Then she caught herself and laughed and said, "Ehh . . . drive any way you want to. We are good at funerals!" Even though she is gone now, I feel closer to her because she said that. Laughter brings us closer together when experiencing common human tragedies. We trust people more when we can laugh with them. Sometimes, you've got to laugh.

I chuckle that Erma Bombeck said the first thing to figure out when you decide to remodel your house is who will get custody of the kids. I had a "mommy brain" when we were remodeling our bungalow, and I was confused by a phone call. The carpenters were working in the house, and my "husband" called and said, "How is everything going?" I had my teenage daughter waiting in the car and said quickly, "It's going fine. I love you, and I'll see you tonight! Bye." No response. Immediately, I knew it was the electrician and not my husband, whom I just planned to see "tonight."

"A good guffaw even decreases stress hormones like cortisol and lowers blood pressure."

I went to the car and told my daughter that I felt like putting a bag over my head. She wisely said I should call back the electrician (who happened to be her boss' brother). So I went back in the house and called on the tan landline with the long stretchy cord (the only phone line in the house). I got his answering machine, into which I completely lost my composure. In breathless laughter, I hung up. He never mentioned it, but his wife told me later she thought it was hilarious when this shy man came home and told her how his day went.

I have long been a fan of asking people to tell me their most embarrassing moment. I love it when I read complaints about pet peeves and gripes in Christmas cards or even complaints in four-part harmony choirs with conductors and orchestral accompaniment. I have been a fan and also a composer of such since a trend-setting choir in Birmingham, England, in 2005, complained about the woes of their hometown. They included how people eat too many biscuits (the British word for cookies) when they have them for tea and how so many bananas don't ripen. It was a fetching performance, posted on YouTube, that spread the idea of Complaint Choirs around the world.

Most countries know how to have a good laugh over their irritating daily hometown dilemmas, with the notable exception of the government of Singapore, which refused a permit for their Complaint Choir. They are missing out on the Laughter Advantage that could save their homes and save them money for health care for their citizens.

For all you science fans, the Laughter Advantage is scientific.

Laughter does cool things in our bodies, like increasing natural killer cells that fight cancer and the number of the famous T-cells in our immune system to fight infection. A good giggle also increases the level of antibodies that fight lots of stuff, including the pesky common cold. A good guffaw even decreases stress hormones like cortisol and lowers blood pressure. How cool is that!? Our bodies and our homes are better off after lightening up with a good laugh.

Home Again Moment

Recently, my husband and I were talking about how many things *haven't* been going right in our house or in our cars. This includes many trips to the auto repair shop and brand-new appliances having to be replaced multiple times. Lou's dad used to tell him that buying extended warranties for anything was just a waste of money! But, we've concluded that we live in the era of planned *early* obsolescence and have learned to do the opposite. While I was having lunch with my husband and cheerfully referencing one of a number of things that hadn't gone right, I made a sound like "ka-kung!" to represent the sound of something *not going right*. We had a big laugh at this made-up sound. Since then, making this sound at the time something goes wrong gives us some healthy emotional release in an otherwise tense moment.

Home Again Questions

What stood out, struck you, or moved you in this chapter?

Think of a time when you were able to see the funny side of something, which, on the surface, was only annoying, but maybe it was worse. What helped you to do that?

For Further Reflection

Laughter is good for us psychologically and physically! That's good news, right? Except, wait—how *often* do we laugh at a joke, notice something humorous, or have enough leisure to have light moments together with friends? When my family and I had a good laugh at ourselves, we were able to see past our pandemic dog's supposed bad points and vote to keep him. We were able to get a fresh viewpoint on the situation. Humor can do that for us! What are the ways you can lighten up your home?

27

Home Telltales

I remembered everything as soon as I grabbed the rudder and looked up at the fluttering telltales that told me the direction of the wind. Telltales are little pieces of fabric that are tied on the edge of the sail that tell the skipper by their fluttering where to steer the rudder. That was a few years ago when my friend Kathy, who had been the captain of the sailing team in college, offered to let me take her small Sailfish boat out on the lake by her cabin north of Eau Claire. It was muscle memory, just like riding a bike. During college, I sailed on Lake Mendota in Madison in the dinghy boats that belonged to the Wisconsin Hoofers Sailing Club. I never had the money to join the club but went as part of a handy, experienced crew with a friend who skippered the boat. We had days of pure delight in the wind and waves.

I have sailboats depicted in art and crafts around our East Hill bungalow, so I remember the feeling of cutting through a wave on a sunny day in a Sunfish, Sailfish, dinghy, or an old yacht of a friend. They remind me to watch the telltales in my home.

When I was 13, after eighth grade, I spent my summer as crew on a two-person team in Snipe races on the Mystic Lakes, with an occasional

Dinghy Regatta on the Charles River in Boston. My "boyfriend," John, would pick me up at my house. Silently, we would walk a mile and a half in the early morning after breakfast to the Winchester Boat Club and practice in one of his father's beautiful Snipe boats. They were sleek wooden racing sailboats with polished wood bows.

This was not really a very romantic relationship. We would break for lunch at the concession window or take a swim in the pool, but mostly, we put on our swimsuits, suntan lotion, and zinc oxide cream across our noses and sailed all day, every day. I think he picked me as his partner because I was very light (about 90 pounds when wet), and it increased his chances of beating his brother, who always came in first before dozens of boats in the Regatta. We were serious, like competitive dance partners, and picking me as his crew was like picking a jockey to ride a prized horse—he wanted to win, or at least to fight for it. My lightness, quick obedience, and trust in his strategy were my contributions to our fight against the wind.

But really, you can't fight the wind. Just accept it and deal with it. Of course, we wanted the wind behind us at a reasonable velocity so we could just put out the sail and catch it, but we knew how to take action and tack with our sail tight as we headed into a gale. Whether we were going upwind, downwind, or moving with the current when there was no wind, the first steps were awareness and acceptance of what our *telltales* were telling us.

I loved to take action when the silence was broken, mostly by intense shouts. "Coming about! . . . Jibe! Put up the spinnaker! Lean starboard! Lean port!" But most of the sailing was quiet acceptance and awareness of the telltales. My sailing experience was mostly of waiting, enduring, trusting in the skipper, and enjoying the newness of each race (since the wind always had its own mind). I enjoyed striving to win, but I also loved letting go and enjoying the sun, admiring the sparkles on the water, and not judging John's disappointment about coming in second every race.

Most of my home experience is a lot like that summer of sailing. There are some actions required, but so much of it is acceptance of things I cannot change and awareness of home telltales that tell me of the ever-changing winds of life. Not everything needs my action! But everything needs my acceptance and nonjudgmental awareness of the people around me. The gale that caused me to lean starboard with all my might and sometimes even to be thrown out of the boat, or the sudden jibe that ended in being rescued after capsizing, or the windless day can all be seen from a perspective of acceptance, awareness, and trust. Yes, action is part of homemaking, but sometimes peacefully treading water while I wait is just what is called for, or ducking low so I am not knocked by the swinging of the boom (the horizontal beam that is attached to the vertical mast at a right angle, which can knock a sailor out of the boat).

"Whether we were going upwind, downwind, or moving with the current when there was no wind, the first steps were awareness and acceptance of what our *telltales* were telling us."

Like sailing, homelife goes better with teamwork, especially when you are "in irons" (which means the boat has stopped and the sail is slack in the windless air), and the usual way of steering with the rudder is useless. Last night, when my husband and I had no wind in our sails after teaching an afternoon class at the university, someone in our home needed to have a serious talk with us. I was "in irons," but my husband was able to gently grab hold of the boom and push the "sail" in the conversation into position to catch just enough wind to make the conversation come to a satisfying end.

That conversation was not one of conflict but just one of tired folks trying to talk about something that needed to be talked about. But then there are some home conversations that involve the fast-changing telltales of the high winds of conflicting viewpoints. Not just awareness and acceptance, but *action* is called for. Not every conflict calls for my blaming judgment—none of them, really. But some call for decisive action and judgment, like a crucial tacking decision of the skipper with a keen eye on the telltales.

And then there are many conversations in the home that just go better with silliness. My brother and I discovered that not all sailing is serious and silly sailing was the most fun, especially the well-timed, forced capsize. As a teen in the '60s, I stood many times laughing together with my brother on the centerboard of a capsized dinghy in the deep, dirty, and fast-flowing water of the Charles River, trying to clamber over the edge of the boat to get enough leverage to recover the upright position. Then, we would quickly bail out the tea-colored water before the Harvard students on river patrol came and kicked us off the water for our repeated shenanigans.

We didn't belong to the prestigious Winchester Boat Club, but the Harvard Yacht Club was free to employees' families. So we sailed in the dirty water in the old clunky dinghies that belonged to Harvard and were "babysat" by the Harvard students as we deliberately created mishaps, breaking sailing rules for fun. Not only had we mastered the forced capsize and recovery, but we even sailed the boats out of bounds by gliding them under the bridge and downriver towards the Boston Harbor.

When my mom became aware of our maritime malarky, she sided with the river patrol that tattled on us. But she did have the presence of mind to get a few funny stories to tell out of it since one of our visiting Midwestern friends, Annie Friedberg, who was soaked while boating with us in the Charles, seemed to be cured of an incurable case of eczema from the famously dirty water. Mom wasn't too worried about our safety. We weren't landlubbers. She knew we were wearing life jackets and could have swum the breadth of that wide river (even with its current) and not even gotten winded. She accepted that some mishaps just happened because we were all trying to have a good time.

I, too, can accept that disputes in homelife happen when everyone is doing their best and trying to have fun. My mom did not have to take much action at all. The telltales told her that she had all the power. We needed her sporting attitude, as she gave a car full of kids a ride from our home in Winchester through the traffic of Harvard Square, so we could enjoy boating on the Charles. She had the power of the car keys. A little disapproval from Mom and peace reigned on the river.

Yes, remembering my days of sailing teaches me that being aware of the subtle telltales of home helps me to decide what combination of acceptance or action is needed. I can be aware of my own part in creating and solving the inevitable conversational mishaps at home and take action only when the telltales are fluttering and there is a need to tack to smooth them. I can lean on other folks who have more wind in their sails, and I can accept with humor the shenanigans, malarky, and occasional capsizing that happens when creative people try to meet their needs for fun and excitement.

And then, there is the dark and stormy night of not-so-fun sailing excitement when the telltales spin and running aground is inevitable. A patient in my little Barstow Street office told me that she had had a traumatic experience the previous week on nearby Lake Wissota when she had gone out sailing alone on a sweltering summer night to ease her mind after a family trauma. An unexpectedly fierce Midwestern thunderstorm caused her to lose control of the little boat and be tossed wildly by high winds toward the dark shore. We discussed how, if she had had the presence of mind, the wisest course was simply damage control by pulling up the centerboard, lowering the sail, and accepting that weather happens. It was a good lesson for her family crisis that required trust and the presence of mind to know when silent damage control would make it easier to recover and heal after the trauma.

Home Again Moment

In this chapter, I recall how my patient and I discussed the parallels between successfully handling a challenging and frightening sailing experience and the wisdom of simply focusing on "silent damage control" and "accepting that weather happens" during family upsets and traumas. Sometimes, doing damage control is the best thing we can do—just making sure a bad situation isn't made worse by our *trying to fix it*.

Home Again Questions

What stood out, struck you, or moved you in this chapter?

As with sailing, sometimes the "telltales" in our relationships with others in our home indicate acceptance, and other times, *action*. Think back on some of the most challenging situations in your homelife. What happened? What helped you decide whether action or acceptance was needed?

For Further Reflection

"Like sailing, homelife goes better with teamwork, especially when you are 'in irons' (which means the boat has stopped and the sail is slack in the windless air)." Think about a time in your homelife when the wind had gone out of your sails, and you tapped into the power of *teamwork*. How did leaning on someone else make a difference?

28

The Little Way of Subtraction

In the mysterious decade of the '50s, when I was 4, I had a private epiphany because I made a Big Mistake. It was an ordinary, warm, sunny morning when I rode my tricycle to the end of our block on Chevy Chase Drive. I was careful to stay on our side of the street because the rule was that I was allowed to ride around the block if I didn't cross a street, so turning left was the correct choice when I came to the cross street.

But at that point, I made a daydreamy mistake. I kept going straight another block to the busy Mattis Avenue and turned left. I was a few houses down when I realized my life-changing mistake. I was completely lost and had failed to memorize my address or my last name. My parents had been working with me on those, but I could not recall either in this emergency. I saw a mom and two children around my age sitting on their front steps. So I turned my trike and drove straight up the sidewalk and explained to the mom that my first name was Ann, and I didn't recall my last name or address.

I inquired, "Can I live with you?"

She was very nice but said, "Keep going."

To be fair to this mom who didn't call social services to report a lost child (like most moms today would do), it was 1956 when the heavy trike and bike traffic of the baby boom was quite common, and not all homes had phones. And the ones that did, had party lines like our house. When you tried to use the phone line, which four other families shared, you usually got a crabby person yelling at you not to listen in. Or if you got a free line, you had to tell the operator lady what number to manually connect the switchboard to. In our city, Champaign-Urbana, this was limited by the number of women downtown hired as operators. But I digress from the existential crisis of the very lost child who was me.

The sadness of the lost child (which I know now is universal and can fall upon us at any age) discolored everything; every house, every yard, and even the sky took on the gray tones of a black and white movie, as I pedaled my tricycle in a mixture of despair and hope. Even the backyard swing sets and sandboxes that I caught glimpses of behind the houses were charmless until I looked at a backyard and recognized the fence that was at the far end of *our* backyard. Through that fence, bespeckled with red cherry tomatoes, I saw *our* little green house, the red wagon, the yellow zinnias, and the rainbow of toys in the sandbox.

I was home, or at least I could see it from there. I dried my tears on my hand, rounded the corners, and rode up the bumpy gravel driveway, parking my trike in the carport.

No one killed the fatted calf. No one had even wondered where I had been. After all, what seemed like forever to me was only a matter of a few minutes' trike ride. For all they knew, I had been dawdling in my dreamy way as I went around the block or was playing in the yard. But I knew I was home again with my family, whom I had lost. A sweet reunion! All the sounds and smells of home, my home, with its smells of floor wax, tuna casserole, cinnamon toast, laundry detergent, and the sounds of work and play, filled up the holes made by the subtraction problem.

"Hi Mom, what is my last name and my address?"

I alone felt the paradoxical epiphany of a subtraction problem. Ann, take away Ann's home equals one, the loneliest number (according to Three Dog Night). My family had been subtracted from my life. And thankfully had been added back in. The experience was like a science-based gratitude exercise we do with our students. We ask them to use their imagination to subtract from their life, their home, their family, and their friends, or anything they treasure. Ponder that, and then add them back into their life. Let that percolate and savor.

"We learn to be patient and treasure the clutter, the chatter, the towel left on the floor, the sand, the smears of peanut butter, the crabgrass, and the dented car."

Sometimes, we learn this well through the mystery of suffering loss in real life. My trike adventure loss was so profound to my life that I remember it in my 70s. Losing a person through death or a loved one through estrangement, or almost losing one through sickness or accident, or so many other ways, can have the counterintuitive effect of causing us to savor the treasures of home, the treasures of people or dear places, or even the very things we found annoying about home. We learn to be patient and treasure the clutter, the chatter, the towel left on the floor, the sand, the smears of peanut butter, the crabgrass, and the dented car. Even as a 4-year-old, my perspective changed. I wonder if my patience with having to eat all my oatmeal or put away my toys was noticeable to my parents.

This cold oatmeal and floor scattered with toys to pick up had almost been subtracted forever because of my own Big Mistake of not paying attention to the rule about not crossing the street and not putting effort into learning my last name and my address as my parents had asked.

The loss of treasured things pierces us all at times in this mortal life, especially if it is because of our mistakes. Out of this *little way of subtraction* came not only my appreciation of others in my home, but also my first recollection of patience with myself. My family helped me to memorize my last name and address (and by the way, I did get it down). I understood that even though I could make a Big Mistake, I was still a valuable person to my family and that I could also feel better if I corrected my mistake.

Home Again Moment

Just like my failure to take my parents' advice to learn my last name or my address led to the dreadful predicament of being cut off from anything and anyone I recognized, so, too, many of our most difficult challenges are, well . . . self-inflicted. Think back on a challenge in your life when neglecting something led to consequences. How did that experience make a difference in your life afterward?

Home Again Questions

What stood out, struck you, or moved you in this chapter?

Recall a time when you lost something precious, treasured, or *necessary* in your life, and then, after twists and turns, you got it back! How did you feel? How did it change you?

For Further Reflection

This chapter mentions an interesting phenomenon: how "losing a person through death or a loved one through estrangement, or almost losing one through sickness or accident" can change our attitude towards the annoying, difficult, or mundane things in our homes and lives to be more accepting and patient. Has this ever happened to you or to someone you know? What did that look like?

29

Hurricane Homemaking: The Other Story

"What a wonderful day!" my husband gushed as he hopped into bed in his flannel pajamas on a recent February night in Wisconsin, with the temperature dropping outside.

I became very curious about his perspective. Because that was not the story I was telling myself about the mundane winter day full of errands, TV, and leftovers.

"What made it so wonderful?" I asked as I straightened the covers.

"The coffee together at Menomonie Market." This is a little grocery store we love that offers an inexpensive cup of coffee, local mushrooms, and sweet workers. From our table, we have a perfect view of the neon sign advertising electric cigarettes across the street.

He had ordered coffee and a savory scone. I had enjoyed my usual: hot water and a banana, as we shared our "profound" thoughts with each other about counteracting the tricks of the mind that make us think our life is a dud. Yes, that was the real topic of conversation as we sat at our tiny table next to our small, fully-paid-for cart of groceries.

To further answer my question about why his day was so wonderful, he went on to say he "loved having lunch together on our sunny porch." This almost 100-year-old porch that we glassed in a few years ago is the size of a cow's stall in a barn but seats six around a little table and has a view of the houses of our street, and a long parade of joggers, school children, families with strollers, and dog walkers going by at various hours of the day. (We try not to notice all the sweaty runners and poop scooping we have in the porch-view.)

"I loved our wonderful dinner." It had been 2-day-old leftover frozen pizza, heated-up Menomonie Market Chicken and Dumpling deli soup, and kale salad eaten in the basement in front of the TV watching *All Creatures Great and Small*. The last episode ends with a Christmas 1940s kissing scene while the young veterinarian and his wife are holding a newborn.

My husband didn't mention the less romantic parts of our "wonderful" day, like paying our mechanic $500 for brake work, etc., on our 2001 Chevy Prizm, or getting a new tube of bacitracin and band-aids for sores on our hands, which we both have from the winter dry weather. Or the cold front coming in, causing us to walk to the auto repair lot to get our silver 2000 Volkswagen Bug out of the way so our beloved (almost retired) mechanic won't have to plow around it when the snow hits tonight—even though it is not fixed yet. (By the way, we are driving it back today or tomorrow after the plowing is done to repair a mysterious German ailment of this geriatric bug.)

But we had a "wonderful day!"

We have a friend who has a podcast called *Tell Me Something Weird*. If I had a podcast, I would love to call it *Tell Me the Other True Story*. I find (in everything that happens in my home) there are two stories: a true story, which I will call *my story*, and well, *the other true story*, after I have a good laugh, good night's rest, or have eaten some chocolate.

This idea of retelling your story highlighting the positive aspects has a fancy technical name that makes it sound boring: *cognitive restructuring*.

"Home is a story we reconstruct after a cup of coffee and a savory scone."

I decided to try the process in the fall of 2012 when I found myself helping my elderly parents during Hurricane Sandy. Here are the two true stories about Hurricane Homemaking. They give you a closer, bird's-eye view into homemaking in the storm.

※○※

My Story:

Hurricane Sandy in Danbury, Connecticut, *was not fun*! The lights went out just as my mom was about to cook some raw chicken, so we had to scramble to find something to eat in the darkened house. The wind was so loud it sounded like a train in the trees when the eye of the storm was 150 miles away. This upset the dog, and he refused to go out to pee for 24 hours.

For a day, the sounds of loud cracking and falling trees could be heard. Aunt Hack Road and Joes Hill Road, the roads connecting us to town, had many downed trees tangled in power lines blocking the roads.

It was very dangerous. Nearby people lost homes and lives. The night turned into morning, and then another night, and another protracted day, with no idea of when life would be normal again.

I spent most of my long days bringing in wood, cooking meals in the fireplace, and standing outside in the wind, trying to get a cell phone connection because I still needed to communicate with my dad's doctors. One time, when he got a bloody nose, I was standing out in the wind, yelling over and over the results of the home blood coagulation test into the phone to the Anticoagulation Clinic's nurse. The connection was so bad we often just showed up at a doctor's office unannounced to have my dad seen. His lungs got really bad from the cold.

Yes, we had snow in October and no furnace. In spite of putting wood on the fire every hour and a half to two hours all night long, my dad was still chilled. Despite having stored some water, bathing and doing dishes in the cold was very difficult. I got stinky, and the dishes piled up. My beloved dad could not use his oxygen tank by the fireside, so breathing was hard for him, especially at night.

The hardest thing about the suffering was *time*. My dad sighed, "The worst part is the uncertainty. We don't have any idea how long this will last." We could have left for a hotel or my brother's house in a nearby state to end this chilly, stinky experience, but my parents didn't want to leave the house vulnerable to looters. And besides, we needed his team of doctors nearby.

The Other True Story:
Hurricane Sandy in Danbury, Connecticut, *was fun*! We had no electricity, running water, heat, landlines, or internet from Monday at 5:45 p.m. until Friday at 1 p.m. We played cards by candlelight and

cooked pork and apples over the fire. We read the newspaper and did the crossword together by a warm hearth. My parents and I and a coon dog named Buddy slept by the fire. We had prepared just enough drinking water and toilet flushing water. We had enough firewood, thanks to neighbors.

Kids who were off school played with toy trucks at our house. We still had trick-or-treaters.

"What can we do to help your parents?" the neighbors asked.

So, I made sure to request something from everyone since many of them had generators. We had deliveries of coffee, hot breakfasts, soup, a cell phone charger, and water. We were invited for dinner and to take showers. We even got help walking the dog and, oh yes, ice to keep our food from spoiling.

I think that if the crisis had only lasted a little longer, the neighbors would have had a bake sale to buy us a generator. Everyone had a story of how my parents had helped them and would not let them do anything back. Well, I changed that. I took everyone up on their offers to help, and we had a great hurricane experience.

The hour of deliverance arrived. The lights suddenly came on, the refrigerator hummed, and the toilets could actually be flushed! We appreciated warm showers as never before! And yes, I wanted to kiss the dishwasher and loved the sweet sounds of the vacuum cleaner and ring of the old landline telephone. My mother took notes on the phone messages that had piled up and read us three pages of caring words from friends and relatives far and near.

Hurricane Sandy caused over eight million people on the East Coast to lose power for days in the cold Fall of 2012, but we were surely experiencing togetherness as never before seen, by me anyway, on Joes Hill in Danbury, Connecticut.

☼☼☼

A 19th-century version of the African American spiritual song (popularized by Louis Armstrong) starts with the line, "Nobody knows the trouble I've seen," and ends with, "Nobody knows the joys I have." Home is a story of trouble *and* joy.

Home is a story we reconstruct after a cup of coffee and a savory scone. It's not that everything is sweetness and light. There is a balanced middle way to look at our homes: a little salt and a little sugar.

Home Again Moment

"Man can alter his life by altering his thinking." —William James. When we find ourselves experiencing more pain than anything else or feeling like we are definitely *not* up to what we're being challenged to be up to, this is when we sure could use some "altering" in our thinking! Perhaps a good way to do this is to ask ourselves—consciously or unconsciously—are there other perspectives I could have? Whether it's a life circumstance or situation, the behavior of another person, or something else. Finding another *perspective* was an important part of my experience during Hurricane Sandy.

Home Again Questions

What stood out, struck you, or moved you in this chapter?

One of the things that helped me tell the "other true story" about Hurricane Sandy was focusing more on the positive things that were a part of my experience and less on the painful things. This takes some effort, but it is worth it! Think of a painful or stressful part of your life. How could you reconstruct your inner narrative about it in a way that turns your experience into the "other true story?"

For Further Reflection

There are a multitude of ways to tell the "other true story." For my husband, focusing on "small" things for

which he was grateful helped turn a very ordinary day in very ordinary circumstances into a "wonderful" day. Some people have a gratitude jar in their home. Other people keep a little notebook by their bed and write down things they're thankful for. A friend of ours told us that every time she says to herself, "Oh no, what if that happens again?" she is in the habit of making herself think of three things that have happened that she is grateful for and then say, "What if *those* happen again?"

30

Home Again and Again

Last night, our family played *Oregon Trail*. It is a game where we pretend we are pioneers in the 1800s trying to get from Independence, Missouri, to Willamette Valley, Oregon, to settle down and make it a home. There are a lot of rivers to ford, diseases to medicate, wagon wheels to fix, and other calamities, but we have supplies and teamwork. After a few tries, we persevere and arrive at our new home, even though we have to have a few burials along the way, from snake bites, dysentery—the usual.

I love to sing the song "Softly and Tenderly." Certainly not as well as Johnny Cash, Elvis Presley, or Cynthia Clawson. It is about the call to come home—the theme song to the 1985 Academy Award-winning movie *The Trip to Bountiful*. Cynthia Clawson's masterful singing of that poignant song moves us as we watch this frail but feisty older woman outwit her overprotective son and persevere to return to her abandoned childhood homestead before she dies. We can feel her longing. She is weary and wants to go home.

I have seen so many people persevere to find ways to get back home again or to make a new place into their home. For example, a woman in her 80s moved out of her house and into her daughter's house. She did this after her doctor diagnosed her with Parkinson's disease and her beloved spouse died the same week. After the funeral, she thought she would be OK staying in her own home, but when her kids went back to their homes, the grief and the worry were too much for her. She called her daughter, "Come pick me up! I can't be alone."

Her daughter drove across Wisconsin to her rural hometown on the eastern side of the state, near Green Bay. Gratefully, her mom got in the car with a bag and went to stay with her in Eau Claire. Her daughter, who knew me from her time in my office during a horrendous divorce, called me. "Can you see my mom a few times a week? My mother's fear and sadness are overwhelming to us. It's too much for me and my teenage daughter to handle."

Even though I never see a patient that frequently, I said, "Yes, let's set up some appointments" because she sounded so desperate to help her mom.

Her children loved her, and all of them were ready for her to move in permanently to their homes. In some cultures, that would have been the natural thing to do, but she was from a community of industrious Wisconsin German farm people, so she prized her self-reliance and enjoyed being independent and busy.

In our first meeting, I said, "Your children would love to have you live with any of them. But what do you want? What do you really, really want?"

"I know my daughter wants me to stay with her, and when she comes home for lunch, it is the highlight of my day, but I am mostly alone. I am so homesick. I want to go home. I am afraid I'm too old and weak. But, I want to try . . . to at least try to go home. At some point, I plan to live with my youngest daughter in Florida and enjoy my grandchildren there, but not yet."

She told me, "I want to go back to my book club and my grief group. I miss my church. I miss my own priest."

She longed for her own world. "I want to go with my friend Dorothy to visit the cemetery. We were planning to make decorations for our husbands' graves and make the trip to the graves together. It is easier to go together. I want to keep making crafts to sell at the town bazaar with my friends. I want to have them over for coffee again and go to potlucks. I've known them since our children were young and some since grade school."

She would wake in the night after dreaming she was in her own house. "I miss my yellow kitchen and the dishes that I got for my wedding. And the roomy bedroom I shared with my husband, even if the stairs to it take me a long time to climb."

"We need another human to take our hand and give us a leg up. Sometimes, we need each other to help us find the strength within us to discover our way home again and again."

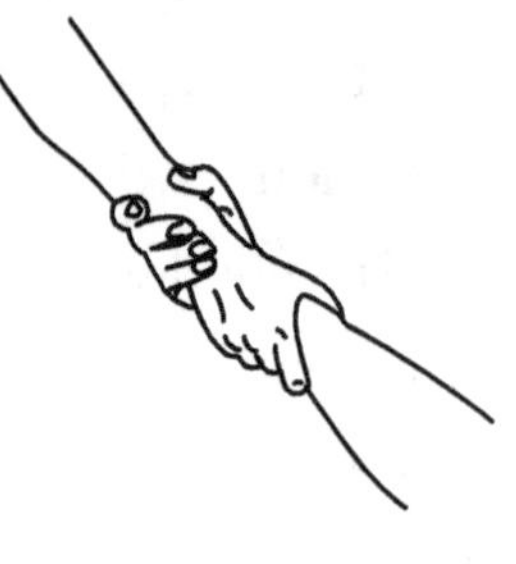

So, meeting with me helped her with planning and baby steps. She would make a realistic goal every session and then she would report how it went. Then, we would tweak the plan as needed.

"Can you help me make phone calls?" she asked. We talked together to the clinic staff in her hometown so she could get her medication adjusted to decrease the side effects.

"Can you help me make appointments?" She started physical therapy so she could manage the stairs to her upstairs bedroom.

"I am so afraid I will fall on the ice!" I helped her contact her town's postal service and started having her mail delivered to her door rather than her roadside mailbox.

"My kids are so afraid I will fall alone in the house, and they won't know." She was willing to wear a button to push if she fell, and we figured out how to set that up.

I knew she was close to her goal when she said, "I started having phone appointments with my hometown counselor. I will miss you so much, Ann, but I hope you won't feel bad if I change counselors to my hometown counselor."

I smiled. "I am happy for you." The big day came, and her daughter drove her home for a 3-day trial period alone in the house. At the end of the trial period, she stayed in her hometown.

She called me to tell me, "My daughter and son came for a weekend and helped me with cleaning and some remodeling to make the stairs and bathroom safer. I'm doing OK. I'm happy to be home. Thank you."

Men and women of all ages find it challenging to get back home again, or to make a new place into their home after a life shock.

I have seen men in my office who, with a few months or a year of support, regain their sense of safety and home after the shock of their girlfriend's or wife's affair. They persevered to make a new home for themselves and their children. Another young man was able to move out of his sister's home and into his own place after he figured out a career path that worked. This was hard after losing the ability to work with his dad. His dad committed suicide. Another got sober and stopped his legal troubles from bar fights that were preventing him from launching from his parents' home and creating his own.

I have seen wonderful, sensitive women learn to get perspective and sort through survivor guilt after a parent's or child's suicide or the murder of a friend, and learn again to focus on their hospitality and nurturing of others in their own homes. I have seen women learn to live in joy and make a beautiful, safe home even though they have been raised in chaos by parents who were plagued by the insanity of alcoholism.

Yesterday, my friend Julia asked me, "Why are some people able to persevere and others aren't?" She is a psychologist who always looks beautiful with her golden-brown hair on top of her head and her warm smile whether she is sitting in her office or walking in the snow to the Court'N House restaurant where our families like to meet. She has worked with many people to help them overcome trauma.

I didn't know the answer to Julia's question. I just thought, "Maybe it's the same reason I am not able to persevere sometimes. I'm too frazzled or tired. I don't know how. I need a gentle person to grab my hand and give me a leg up. I'm not myself. I need to come to myself as an old, compassionate friend. I need to rest enough to remember how to eat an elephant, one bite at a time."

I'm not sure of the full answer to Julia's question. But my patients have taught me that just as there is a natural law of sickness and loss that causes us all to sink under the power of grief and sometimes fail, there is a counterbalancing natural law. Within each human that I have met, there is a unique set of *strengths* that can be harnessed to get better, to get home again, or to adjust to a new home.

Some of my patients had the strength of humility, others the strength of self-regulation, others the strength of faith, some were really organized, and others found humor everywhere. I have seen so many strengths that made all the difference in their ability to persevere.

Tina, my mentor, told me of the tearfully joyful time she had in her office with a family as their depressed teenager realized her strengths. Tina had asked the parents to look over a list of strengths and pick out their child's strengths, and the parents told the child of the beautiful strengths they saw.

"You are honest, a good problem solver, and so creative. You care about people's feelings."

Tears rolled down her face as she began to see how she could get unstuck.

I think part of the answer to Julia's question about why some people persevere is that some people use their strengths. In my cozy, sunny office, drinking herbal tea and sitting in cushioned wicker chairs, I listen intently as the patients tell me about the trouble that brought them to talk to me. After they explain to me how they have gotten stuck, I often say things like:

"Tell me about your strengths."

"Who do you know who also has these strengths?"

"Are there ways you can follow that person's example in handling the troubles that you are going through?"

"How have you used these strengths in the past?"

We all get lost, get far from home, get in the weeds. In our humanness, we look at other people's outsides and think we are the first person or only person that feels this lost.

We need another human to take our hand and give us a leg up. Sometimes, we need each other to help us find the strength within us to discover our way home again and again.

Home Again Moment

"Men and women of all ages find it challenging to get back home again, or to make a new place into their home after a life shock." Can you think of a time when a shock happened in your life? Or when an even smaller version of this happened to you? What was it? How did you cope with it?

Home Again Questions

What stood out, struck you, or moved you in this chapter?

"Within each human that I have met, there is a unique set of *strengths* that can be harnessed to get better, to get home again, or to adjust to a new home."

Think of a time when you were coping with sickness, loss, grief, or other painful circumstances that caused you to lose the sense of security, peace, settledness . . . *home*. Or a time when you were in a new home that was, well . . . too new yet to be of comfort to you.
How did you manage? What were your strengths that helped you?

For Further Reflection

"We all get lost, get far from home, get in the weeds . . . Sometimes, we need each other to help us find the strength within us to discover our way home again and again."

What was a time in your life when you were suffering, and you felt like you were the first or only person who was suffering the exact way that you were? What a lonely, painful place that is!

Think of a time like this in your life when the right person was there for you at the right time. Describe your experience. Or, if right now you are suffering and feeling lost, who is a gentle person in your life to whom you can turn today?

Afterword

Yesterday, our latest model grandchild (numero six) was babbling on her mother's lap. She reminded me of the little red-headed house finch we saw that day contentedly eating in an apple tree. Even with a post-nap tear on her face, she had a song to sing and was singing it! She was offering no goods or services to the household and had no idea how happy she made others. But she knew she was *beloved*. May she carry with her the deep muscle memory of relaxing in her mother's arms or being entertained for hours by her laughing older siblings and being beloved. May this sense of being beloved be a protection to her in the inevitable troubles in life that come to us all.

In our bungalow, we have a framed painting on the wall of a room we call the "cozy room," given to me by a single father whose wife came to have schizophrenia after they had children. The painting is of a river in the wilderness.

This homemaking business is not for cowards.

He is the breadwinner, homemaker, protector, and river in the wilderness for his children and wife. Their house is full of love, pets, yummy meals, relatives who come to visit, and a beautiful garden. Bending over his garden, with dirt on his hands and wind-blown blond hair, he often looks handsome but tired. Yes, I can imagine a world where love requires no sacrifice, no pain, but that is not his world. It is not our world here on this planet.

When I look up and see the painting he painted of *The River in the Wilderness* on the wall over our little couch, it speaks to me of home again and again. Of what, at times, seems to be the impossible challenge of making a home here on Earth in what can feel like a wilderness. I look around at my family, neighbors, and people who work in group homes, hospitals, and classrooms and I am inspired by their perseverance of homemaking in the wilderness that is our world, where so many things go wrong. I want to say "thank you" for inspiring these pages!

That way in the wilderness is made by *love and sacrifice*, which are always bound together in our world. My husband has demonstrated this loving sacrifice lately in minor ways, like not complaining while changing the batteries in all the smoke alarms, as he is starting to feel better after a life-threatening adventure. And in major ways by being peaceful and trusting during ER trips and not complaining about emergency cardiac surgery and subsequent pain.

In this book, I have tried to capture elements of home, yet no one can truly distill what home means, for it is so much more than all these elements, just as light is so much more than all the colors of the spectrum. It is a glittering, glimmering energy, mighty and gentle, unspeakably beautiful, that makes all it touches illuminated. Just as home is.

Acknowledgments

First, I want to thank my children, grandchildren, and future great-grandchildren who inspired this book and for whom it is written.

By myself, I would not be able to write a book about home, let alone make a home. Of course, the people who have influenced this book the most are my family, who are in this book. Yet there are so many more—so many homes that have changed my understanding of homemaking in gentle ways. Your homes have inspired me to write this book, and your presence in my home has shown me what really makes a home.

I also thank Dr. Rebecca Meacham at the UW–Green Bay Teaching Press for believing in my book, and her wonderful students: project manager Allie Wendricks; book co-designers Caleigh Cleary and Emily Heling; chief copyeditors Katrina Gebert and Kephren Pritchett; developmental editors Aidann Woodcock, Isaac Azevedo, and Aubrey Laux; style guide co-lead Ruth Drew; marketing leads Paige Hartmann, Kaitlyn Yonke, Dylan Nessman, and Annaliese Gagnon; and copyeditors Trinity Cottrell, Tierney Dewane, Ariel Rutten, Autumn Johnson, Kayla Kluth, Paige Hartmann, and Sam Duits. Their help and encouragement were gold to me, and I am deeply indebted to them.

Of course, thank you to all beta readers (at UW–Green Bay and beyond), especially friends and experts in writing who helped make this readable and encouraged me to be myself: Erik, Judy, Randi, Julia, Carol, Ron, Jane, Rob, Danielle, Claire, and Patti.

And thank you so much, Judy and Carol, for providing photos. Last, but not least, I am thankful to my husband Lou, who worked long hours with me on this book and, even when I doubted it, believed it needed to be published so it could be shared way beyond my original vision of family and friends.

FORGIVENESS HANDOUT

Please use it freely. An electronic version can be found at
http://www.holistictherapyllc.com

Guideposts to Forgiveness

Holistic Therapy LLC (Dr. Ann Recine) & Lou Recine Coaching LLC, 2022 ©

Where the forgiveness guideposts come from: The guideposts below come from interviews by nurses with many people who changed their lives through forgiveness. These people were hurt by what often would seem unforgivable. They were justifiably angry but found the power to let go of that anger. The words below express the ideas and example of these people who found a way to live lives of peace and joy in spite of being hurt.

1. Understand your hurt. Before you can forgive yourself or another person, you need to examine what happened to you—what led up to the event, who did what, and acknowledge that it was unjust and hurt you. Then, you need to recognize your feelings. It's okay to feel sad, lonely, irritable, anxious, or angry. It is important to understand how it's affecting your health, your body, energy level, concentration, or sleep.

2. Begin with knowledge. Know the definition of forgiveness. Forgiveness is letting go of your anger and resentment (even though justified) and choosing to have a positive intention towards the person who hurt you. It is not letting the person off the hook legally, nor is it forgetting or pretending that it didn't happen, nor deciding you're going to hang out and be friends. Forgiving does not mean giving up safety or personal boundaries.

3. Press pause. There are ways to learn how to gently stop the noisy circles of angry, painful thoughts in your mind. You can find a quiet place and time to calm yourself. Take time to figure out how you want to respond instead of reacting.

4. Put your health first. Know that the health of your body is connected to the health of your mind. Your health is more important than your hurt. Give yourself the gifts of health, peace of mind, and happiness that come from letting go of anger.

5. Take baby steps. Know that forgiveness and feeling better takes time. It starts with being willing to be willing to forgive. It begins with wanting to get your life back—with wanting to be at peace.

6. Change channels. We might not be in control of our thoughts initially, but we can learn to shift our focus. When you are angry or upset, you have the option to pick a more peaceful channel. You can think of what you are grateful for today. You can notice the pleasant and beautiful things in your life. You can focus on lifting someone else up today.

7. Power-up. When your mind slips back into focusing on the hurt and hurtful person, and you feel powerless over your angry feelings, reach out to a power greater than yourself. Notice what gives you strength and inspires hope that you can lead a happier, peaceful life in spite of having been hurt. Develop a practice of meditation, prayer, spiritual reading, religious services, or anything else that connects you to that source of power.

8. Lean on somebody. Don't be afraid to ask a strong, trustworthy person in your life for help. Choose to lean on people who care about you and are forgiving.

9. See both sides. Think about a time when you have hurt someone in a way that was against your values. Deeply understand what was going through your mind and the pressures you were under. Seek to

understand the kinds of pressures and struggles the person who hurt you was experiencing.

10. Look for meaning. There will come a day when you will be able to find the good that has come to you as a result of growing from the hurtful experience—and even find the good in the other human being who hurt you. Let the virtues that you value help you make sense of the hurtful experience and achieve forgiveness as a personal victory.

11. Realize life is short. We don't know how many days we have left. Is there an attitude you would be willing to give up in order to have peace inside? It's empowering to take charge of a relationship by deciding to forgive. By choosing to forgive, you are showing people what you value and how you'd like to be remembered.

12. Forgive yourself. You are human, vulnerable, and you make mistakes. Self-forgiveness is something you learn by understanding your own feelings and the feelings of others in a non-judgmental way. Whether the cause of the trouble is your responsibility or someone else's, or a combination, you can approach yourself with compassion and a gentle determination to change for the better. That change may include a new pattern of behavior, setting new boundaries, and new ways to care for yourself and others.

About the Authors

Ann Gentry Recine is a mom, grandmother, sibling, and wife. She is also a college teacher and a retired nurse. Her long fascination with all things home inspired the essays found here. She treasures her life in Wisconsin (the place she has called home now for many years) and her memories of growing up in Illinois and New England.

Lou Recine is Ann's husband. He is also a dad, grandfather, and Ann's research partner, co-author, and co-presenter at seminars and in university classes. His experience in quality assurance, publishing, and as a life coach was invaluable to the writing of this book. Together with Ann, they have two children and seven grandchildren.

In 1945, Army Captain George Snow (the dad from chapter 13) took this picture: the first sight of home for weary U.S. troops.